THE DR. DREW *and* ADAM BOOK

So You Think You Know It All? Don't Miss What Adam and Dr. Drew Say About...

- The Latest Trends in Experimenting with Sex
- Why Guys Are So Worried About the Size of Their Penis
- Internet Relationships—Do They Ever Work Out?
- Are There Places You Shouldn't Get Tattooed?
- What Piercing Different Parts of the Body Says About You
- How to Know if You're Masturbating Too Much
- What Guys Find Sexy in Women . . . and What Really Turns Women On
- The Truth About Female Orgasm
- How to Help a Friend Who's Depressed . . . and Other Dead Serious Issues
- **Plus** Adam and Dr. Drew's Personal Rating System, or PRS, that Measures Your Attractiveness to Others on a Scale of One to Ten

THE DR. DREW *and* ADAM BOOK:

A Survival Guide to Life and Love

DREW PINSKY, M.D.,

and ADAM CAROLLA

with

Marshall Fine

A Dell Trade Paperback

THE DR. DREW *and* ADAM BOOK

A SURVIVAL GUIDE TO LIFE and LOVE

A DELL TRADE PAPERBACK
Published by
Dell Publishing
a division of
Bantam Doubleday Dell Publishing Group, Inc.
1540 Broadway
New York, New York 10036

BOOK DESIGN BY AMANDA DEWEY

Library of Congress Cataloging in Publication Data
Pinsky, Drew.
The Dr. Drew and Adam book: a survival guide to life and love / Dr. Drew and Adam Carolla, with Marshall Fine.
p. cm.
ISBN 0-440-50836-3
1. Love—Miscellanea. 2. Sex—Miscellanea. 3. Man-woman relationships—Miscellanea. I. Carolla, Adam. II. Fine, Marshall, 1950– . III. Title
HQ801.P59 1998
306.7—dc21 98-16472
CIP

Printed in the United States of America
Published simultaneously in Canada
November 1998
10 9 8 7 6 5 4 3 2 1

To my wife, Susan, without whose love and support none of this would have been possible.

—Dr. Drew Pinsky

Yeah, me too.

—Adam Carolla

Acknowledgments

The authors would like to acknowledge the contributions of Howard and Maria Lapides, without whom this book would not have been possible.

Also, Chip Butterman at Lapides Entertainment; David Stanley and Scott Stone at Stone/Stanley Productions; CBS; MTV; Mort Janklow, Tina Bennett and Bennett Ashley at Janklow & Nesbit Associates; Thomas Patrick Rowan, Esq.; Bruce Lagnese at Mucci & Lagnese; and Tom Spain and Jacob Hoye at Dell.

Special thanks to: Donny Brown; Jon Cryer; Greg Camp; Kevin Coleman; A.J. Dunning; Janeane Garofalo; Jennifer Grey; David Alan Grier; Steve Harwell; Caroline Rhea; French Stewart; Ice T; Brian Vander Ark; Keenen Ivory Wayans; and Marlon Wayans.

Marshall would like to thank Rick Fine, John Fiscus, Gus Silva and Diane Netara. He would also like to thank his wife, Kim, and his sons, Jacob and Caleb.

Contents

THE DR. DREW *and* ADAM BOOK

Introduction

The Polar Bear Theory

Q: Can you explain your "polar bear theory" of human behavior?

Adam: It's like this: When you want to study a species, you don't need to examine each and every one of them. To study how polar bears mate and interact, to learn what they eat or if they're territorial, you don't have to study every polar bear. It's going to take only about 50—

Dr. Drew: —to learn how they behave when something happens to them.

Adam: By watching a representative group, you can figure out what you can expect most polar bears to do in a given situation. And the same is true of people. I've always felt that humans are just like any other species on the planet. If you study a representative group of people, you can pretty much predict how all people will react. People are all the same.

So if you get molested as a kid, then you become an abuser or a victim your whole life. That's it. People's responses to these things just aren't that different. But people seem to think there's a different rule book for every person. Absolutely not.

Dr. Drew: This country has a problem with the notion of free will disorders. "Hey, it's a free country—you can do what you want." Free to do whatever. And you know what?

Adam: You're free to paint your house whatever color you want. But emotionally—

Dr. Drew: Emotionally, you're free to act out, is all you're free to do. And you will act out in a way that is highly predictable. But people have real difficulty accepting that.

Q: What are the tip-offs that someone has a much larger problem than the one they're willing to admit to?

Dr. Drew: It's almost something you can hear in their voice.

Adam: The little-girl-voice thing is one of the ways we know. Women in particular, when they get abused, tend to arrest their development at age 12 and their voice sounds like a twelve-year-old even when they are twenty-five.

Dr. Drew: There is a mixture between "Don't you want to love me?" and real hostility.

Q: How hard is it to get people to see what the real problem is?

Dr. Drew: Intellectually, it's pretty easy to get people to see it because it's so obvious. Getting past their defenses is another story.

Adam: You can show somebody the brain tumor on their CAT scan and they can understand it. They can't get a mirror and the scalpel and fix it themselves. But show them a problem in their relationships, and they don't want to go through the process of getting it taken care of.

Dr. Drew: It's like the girl who says, "I've been going out with this guy for a while but we have this problem," and can't figure out that problems in her past are affecting relationships in the present.

Adam: But that's what happens. It's like a tumor that doesn't kill you. People don't realize how much work it is to get over the things that happened to them when they were younger, whether it was abuse or whatever. It's easier to ignore than work at. So it's like having cancer: You say to someone, "Look, you've got to go through this chemo, your hair's going to fall out, you're going to start vomiting, you're going to become emaciated, and your life is going to be turned inside out for six months or a year." That gets their attention and they say, "Is this tumor going to kill me?"

But if the answer is "No, it's just going to kind of dull your senses, there will be a little pain, it's going to make it difficult to concentrate," the person will say, "I can live with that."

Sure, it puts a little pressure on the part of your brain that is in charge of relationships, sexuality, you might get the wrong guy, but you'll never know it. They're thinking, I can beat this thing on my own. Like, if they just read a book or—

Dr. Drew: Or talk to their friends. Or see a psychic. Go to Scientology if things get real bad.

Adam: People have this misconception that the mind heals like the body. Like, you got some kind of laceration at the age of eight; by the time you're nine, it will be all healed. The mind doesn't heal like the body. In fact, it works on the opposite principle, which is a really confusing thought, because all these things that happen to you physically seem to get better, especially when you're younger. They seem to sort of work themselves out as the years or weeks wear on. But emotionally, it never works that way.

Dr. Drew: Well, it does work in the sense that you gain distance from the pain. The pain heals. But there is a consequence for that, because the people start adjusting their whole relationship with reality as a way of avoiding that pain. They end up abandoning pieces of themselves. In their adult life, they reenact their childhood by developing relationships with people who represent the activity that went on when they were in childhood. And, of course, the cast is made up of abusive people, just like the cast was when they were a child. The problem is you can't have it both ways.

Adam: The way I see it, either you mess people up or you don't. I always look at kids like a new car. It's like all you can do is hit a pothole or back up into a parking meter. You've got this new, beautiful car—all you can do is screw it up. Once in a while you get some owner who puts some synthetic oil in it; he gets a LoJack and a car cover; and he puts some rims and tires on. But once in a while, even he'll screw it up a little.

Q: Do people always assume their problems are unique?

Adam: A lot of this society is built on the idea that you, as an individual, are special and different. Watch any sneaker or douche commercial—for guys, it's the sneakers; for women, it's the hygiene products. If you watch them, they'll constantly explain how there's nobody like you. You're different. You deserve this and you deserve that.

So having us tell people they're all the same and react the same way to the same things is somewhat insulting and disappointing to them at times.

Dr. Drew: We aren't saying everybody isn't unique as a person—just that their conduct and behavior and reaction to different emotional events cause certain behaviors that can be very predictable.

Q: Why try to put this kind of information into a book?

Adam: It gives us a chance to organize our thoughts a little, to edit ourselves a little bit.

Dr. Drew: We aren't trying to be perfectly accurate from a medical standpoint. But we are trying to provide a reference point for the people who read it.

Q: What is the message that you're trying to get across?

Dr. Drew: Don't have kids.

Adam: Yes, our new slogan is "Only nuns should have children."

No, what we're trying to say is that no matter how young or how stupid you are—and sometimes they're the same thing—what you do has consequences. Whether it's that first hit of crack or that first shot of heroin or that first attempt at unprotected sex, there's a definite possibility of its affecting the rest of your life. Just because you're sixteen doesn't mean you can't have a baby. Just because you're sixteen doesn't mean you can't have a crack habit. Just because you're sixteen doesn't mean you won't make that trip to the liquor store on your motorcycle without a helmet and wind up a vegetable the rest of your life.

Dr. Drew: Your actions do have consequences. We hope that people who read the book get that message loud and clear.

Q: Anything else you hope people get out of it?

Dr. Drew: That you can shape your own future, no matter how ugly your past has been. Whether you were abused or neglected or whatever problems you have.

Adam: You're not doomed to spend the rest of your life acting out. You can change your life—and I'm not talking about a nose job or a boob job. I'm talking about remaking your emotional life, creating a new you. You aren't sentenced to spend the rest of your life reliving your childhood if you're willing to make the effort to change your life. But it's a slow process and it takes a lot of work.

1

The Difference Between Genders

Q: Is there a secret guys need to know to understand women sexually?

Adam: I hate to sound crass but the reason they call it pussy is because, well, it's like, you can handle a cat like you handle the vagina—here's the deal. A cat is really a vagina with paws.

If you approach the vagina like you approach a cat, see, a cat will let you know immediately. If you goose the cat or you smack the cat, it's out of there. Take a cat—and I don't get an erection or anything around cats, it's just an analogy—you can't go against the fur grain. You can't just grab its head. That's why a cat never hangs out with a kid, because a kid grabs the ear and starts bending it in weird directions—and the thing is out of there.

First off, you have to approach a cat slowly or you can't even really approach it.

You can't go running up to it. It's out of there. Same with the vagina. You can't charge at the vagina—you have to move in slowly. Put your hand out, let it sniff it a little bit, make sure everything is cool. Then even move in and wait for the vagina to come in to you a little bit, you know what I mean—sort of work rhythmically, no poking, no roughhousing, no going against the grain, don't change things up all the time, establish a little pattern. The cat will let you know by starting to lean in a little bit.

Dr. Drew: People ought to practice on cats.

Adam: They really should. People are going to take this the wrong way and think we're doing weird things to cats.

Dr. Drew: Use only your hand when practicing on a cat.

Adam: A cat will let you know by purring, by becoming more relaxed, more settled in your lap. Let's say it's on your lap and you're doing something it doesn't like—you can feel it sort of tense up a little, getting ready to bolt off the lap. And women are the same way.

In fact, I was thinking: Men should approach the vagina like a cat and women should approach the penis like it was a big black Labrador at the beach. Throw that stick, let it jump for it, let it go back, and then when it comes back, roll it down on its belly and grab it by the scruff of the neck, shake it around a little bit, grab its ears and sort of tug on them.

Dr. Drew: The question is, how do you get the Lab and the cat together?

Adam: That's the thing. The Lab will overpower the cat, knock it over. The cat will try to avoid it.

Dr. Drew: The cat's not happy. And this is the soul of the interpersonal experience right here. A black Lab and a large Persian cat.

Q: Do men and women approach relationships differently?

Dr. Drew: Absolutely. Because they approach sex differently.

Q: What's the difference?

Dr. Drew: Women have an emotional experience and connection through sex that they can't easily let go of. They're bewildered when a man can.

Men have a more visual, external experience to their sexuality. You don't see a porn industry for women—you see it for heterosexual and gay males. It's only men who are driven to consume that visual experience. For guys, the purely sexual experience can be gratifying. To a guy, sex is more often about the physical act.

For a female, there's a little more involved in the decision to have sex. The way they experience it is something totally different. They tend to experience it as an emotional, connected, intimate experience. Women have trouble accepting that, for a man, it is often a mechanical, visual, detached experience. They really need to understand that there's a biology operating here that doesn't motivate men toward higher good.

DR. DREW on a Key Difference Between Men and Women

According to a story told about President Calvin Coolidge, he and his wife were visiting a government-run farm one day and they decided to tour the facility separately. As Mrs. Coolidge passed the chicken coop, the guide explained to her that the rooster copulated dozens of times each day. To which she replied, "Please tell that to the president."

When the president was being shown the same coop, the guide felt obligated to repeat Mrs. Coolidge's remark about the fact that the rooster had sex dozens of times a day. Coolidge asked, "Is it with the same hen every time?" Told no, he responded, "Please tell *that* to Mrs. Coolidge."

The point is that even with millions of years of evolution behind us men still have the instinct to spread their genes to as many females as possible and can do it with a wide number of women, seemingly without problems. But to the female, accepting those genes—and bearing a child—is such a commitment that the female wants some longer-standing connection with the male in order to take on that responsibility. Men's relationships can be rapidly changing and unstable; the female wants something more secure and supportive. Emotional differences aside, that's one of the genetic differences between the two genders.

Q: I've been going out with this guy for a while. We seemed to be getting along really well, but he tells me he only wants to be friends even though we have great sex. What should I do?

Dr. Drew: This is at the core of male/female view of sexuality. You hear so often that the man can be totally detached emotionally while having sex, while a woman can't believe that he couldn't be sharing some kind of an emotional experience when she's having one. And you know, if he says he only wants to be friends, believe him. He's telling you the truth. And he's not going to suddenly fall in love.

Q: Why can't women approach sex the same way as men?

Dr. Drew: Because women want something more. But they're being told that they don't need anything else.

It is the fundamental idea that they experience physical intimacy the same way. That's what our society tells us. That was the message of the sexual revolution: We are equal, it's all the same.

And it's not the same. It is NOT the same.

The sexual revolution—particularly the fact that women could have sex without fear of pregnancy, thanks to the birth-control pill—was never thought through in terms of teaching young women how to create stability in a relationship and find fulfillment in a relationship; it was all about having sex in the same way men have sex.

Women's brains are set up differently. But the whole women's movement maintains there's no difference between the sexes, which is a mistake. Women are the ones who get sold short. They expect they can be the same as men in relationships. But they have different needs and those needs have to be protected.

Women shouldn't expect to be able to behave like a man or to be gratified when they do.

For men, it's usually a mechanical act; it can be very unemotional. The biology points toward genetic diversity, to multiple partners. With a man, the commitment is to the physical encounter.

Adam: My take is a little different. It's not so much that all men think about is sex but that they think about themselves a lot. And part of thinking about yourself is thinking about you getting it on. To me, that's about yourself. I mean, it's not just all about sex, sex, sex. It's about you and someone else. It's about you and business, you and someone else having sex. This is why guys make worse parents. And it comes out in terms of sex, but really, when you think about it, guys are just doing their thing.

Dr. Drew: It's usually an aggressive, outwardly projecting thing. Outside the home, outside the self. It's a projection outward that women don't naturally, biologically, do.

Adam: A man can make a career of one-night stands. Sure, there are a lot of decent guys out there, but even decent guys still think about having sex regularly and that sex doesn't necessarily attach to a relationship.

Here's all you need to know about men. Why does it seem like every young rock musician and movie star gets himself into trouble with the ladies? Because he can.

Tips on Living Together for the First Time

I believe a relationship is good for a certain number of days. So when you live together, you use those days up all at once. You can see each other twice a week for four years—or live together for six months.

Things you never noticed before suddenly become glaringly apparent. You don't notice those things when you see each other only on the weekends, but when you start living together—watch out.

One problem is that women see a relationship like a soap opera. They don't want to miss a single day. But a guy isn't into it every day. A guy might think he loves pizza—but let him eat it every day for two weeks and see how committed he is to pizza.

So here are a few tips.

For guys: Think of a relationship like a car: There's always maintenance that needs to be done or things start to fall apart. Whether it's an '87 Honda or a Lamborghini, you have to keep on it. If you don't replace the timing belt, then the piston is going to break the connecting rod and then you've got real trouble.

You've got to watch a relationship like a doctor watches a tumor—you've got to monitor it all the time. You can't let it take over. If you leave it alone, before you know it, all you can do is put a bullet in it. You have to be on high maintenance.

There's a whole side that has to do with responsibility. That means staying on top of the basics: cleaning, shopping, paying the bills. If you don't, it only adds fuel to the emotional stuff. If you ignore those things, she's got a whole new reason to be pissed off.

For women: You have to realize that, when they start living together with you, guys are out of their natural habitat. At the zoo, if you see a monkey or a polar bear, the zoo makes a feeble attempt to mimic their habitat. Now, to the animals, there's a certain advantage to being in the zoo. They're fed at a certain time, they don't have to worry about being eaten by a hyena. On the other hand, they're not out there swinging from tree to tree.

So you've got to be like the zookeeper and feed them their food and make them think they're back in the jungle, even if they're in a cage.

Which means this: When you move in together, don't put on the full-court press. Don't say, "I know you've played softball every Thursday night for the past eight years. This has to end." That's like taking the tire swing out of the monkey cage. The last thing you want is the monkey up in the cage shaking the bars. The softball game is the guy's tire swing. Don't pull the drawstring on a thing that already feels confining.

Q: Why can guys be satisfied with one-night stands and porno, and women can't?

Adam: Women like visual aids, too. But for them, they're just that—aids. For the guy, they can be the whole experience—and he can be happy with it.

Here's how guys think. If you show a guy a picture of Cindy Crawford, his first impulse is, "This is a great-looking woman."

His second impulse is, "Boy, I'd like to have sex with her."

Then somebody tells him, "Well, you can't because she's too smart and too rich and she lives too far away."

So his next impulse is, "If I can't have sex with her, I sure would like to see someone else having sex with her."

It's almost like a reductive thing, trying to get the closest approximation to the physical experience. What he's thinking when he sees some other guy with Cindy Crawford is, *It could be me.*

But for women, the closest thing to the act that's gratifying are the feelings attached to it. When women masturbate, they think about being with a person and the feelings attached to that person. It's not a visual experience. That's why women don't masturbate in front of a VCR.

Dr. Drew: Women consistently find themselves in terribly painful circumstances as a result of doing what a man wants in order to snare the man into a relationship. Almost without exception, these relationships end with the women feeling severely compromised.

Women can't understand how men can engage in physical intimacy without having an emotional experience. Women usually have a very intense emotional experience when they have sex. But women aren't prepared for that by our culture. They're told they should be like men, that they should be able to have multiple partners and anonymous sex without feeling bad about it. And when they feel bad, it confuses them; they think there's something wrong with them—when, in fact, they should trust those feelings.

★ *from Actor French Stewart*

Q: I give my girlfriend oral sex all the time, but she won't do it to me. What can I do?

★ **French:** As a rule, there's a certain give and take that's usually expected. But also, as a rule, I think it's best not to make somebody do something that they don't want to do sexually. Anytime you start getting into talking somebody into doing something they obviously don't want to do, I think it just goes bad.

Adam: Yeah, especially when it's one of those service industries. Look at it this way: You want a massage from somebody. But they're tired, they don't want to do it—maybe they have carpal tunnel syndrome. Now, if you force them to give you a massage, how good is that massage going to be?

★ **French:** Absolutely.

Adam: Women don't provide this service for a host of reasons. And sometimes it's because they were traumatized at some age, and sometimes it's because they are just not thoughtful partners. But a lot of times, they think they are going to screw it up and they're self-conscious. We talk to women all the time who say, "I'd like to do this, but I'm kind of embarrassed. I'm scared he's not going to like it. I don't have much experience doing this and I don't feel comfortable because I don't know what I am doing." To which the correct response is always, "Listen, you can do no wrong. No one is going to laugh at you; effort is all we're really asking for here."

★ **French:** I think talking honestly about what you're thinking will usually solve a lot of your problems. If you can actually talk to somebody, and it sounds so cheesy, but usually you can get to the bottom of what's going on and then make your call. I think you just have to ask her.

Dr. Drew: You have to question her very carefully about what the problem is. If she just finds that totally abhorrent or distasteful, you may just have to accept that. People shouldn't be forced to do things they really find unpleasant.

Adam: And give her an option. You don't have to try to trick somebody into something. You can say, "Hey, this is something that I really enjoy and it's a part of the experience. What do you say?"

★ **French:** I find that when you go to the Dairy Queen, if you don't put in an order, you don't get your parfait.

Q: If men and women are different, are all women the same—and all men?

Adam: Here's my feeling. I think females have the ability to run the gamut sexually more than men do.

Dr. Drew: What does that mean? You mean be aggressive?

Adam: Look at it this way. You talk to your average fifteen-year-old male, you're going to get the same guy pretty straight through. You talk to your average twenty-year-old male, pretty much going to get the same guy. Go to any college campus in this country, walk into a fraternity or a dorm, find a twenty-one-year-old guy, you're getting the same guy.

Dr. Drew: In terms of their interpersonal conduct, yes.

Adam: But go to a college and find women who are twenty and you're going to find the gamut: women who are virgins, women who've been with one man the whole time, who don't believe in this or that. You're going to find women who are multiorgasmic, who've been at parties with three guys—

Dr. Drew: You're going to find women who are sexually promiscuous and feel bad about it, women who are promiscuous and feel good about it—

Adam: Right. And this is as much evidence as you need to know that, as far as men go, sex is a biological deal. It's just biology. But, for a woman, it's much more psychological.

Q: Is it true that men want sex and women want relationships?

Adam: I think there's a lot of women out there who, if they could get a guy with ambiguous genitalia to just sort of lie on them and essentially hump them without using his penis, they'd probably be happy with that. I mean, let's say a guy with no penis got on top of a woman and did the whole process minus the insertion, there's a large percentage of women who'd go for that. The insertion part is just a good excuse to get a guy to lie on top of them and caress them and hold them and make love to them. What I mean is, we talk to a lot of women, a larger percentage than not, who don't have an orgasm through intercourse.

Dr. Drew: Right. It's probably more common than not.

Adam: What's really in it for a lot of them is the holding and what's in it for a guy is that he gets to put his dick somewhere.

Dr. Drew: But a guy thinks that's what a girl wants. Hey, that's what feels good to him and so therefore that must be what feels good to her.

Adam: He thinks she wants the dick part—

Dr. Drew: —because that's what feels good to him.

Adam: But it's really the attention and the caressing.

Dr. Drew: Now if a woman gets all the attention and emotional connectedness that she's looking for, unfortunately most women delude themselves into believing that, just because a guy is doing that, that he is emotionally available. And, most of the time, they're not. They're just doing it for the sex.

A woman will be more fulfilled with the intercourse; I believe that. Intercourse is an important part of it for a woman. But part of the instinct they have is for childbearing. Their fantasy is about procreating and the kind of intimate, erotic feeling attached to that for a woman. For a man, it's not that at all. It's about the physical, visual experience. Although they can be gratified by sex, to be fulfilled they have to be led into intimacy by the woman.

Q: What causes those differences?

Dr. Drew: It's biological. Women have a predominant sexual hormone called estrogen that makes them sort of passive and receptive in their sexuality. Their biology is not directing them to be assertive and aggressive. When they have intercourse, women also release a hormone called oxytocin, which makes them more susceptible to the urge to bond.

A man, on the other hand, has all this testosterone. So he is being driven to extreme aggression.

Q: How does a woman learn to tell a man what she wants?

Adam: Well, women should not be trying to trick men. They should be trying to train men. A book like *The Rules* basically tells women, "Here's how to trick a man into marriage" or a second date or whatever. Well, you can trick them temporarily, until they regain their senses.

Look at it this way: A dog would rather use the doggie door than jump through the screen or make a mess on the floor and get in trouble. It's your job to show him which door to use and when. Men are happier when they're housebroken.

Dr. Drew: Women are the keepers of intimacy. Humans are gratified by intimacy. But we men are pathetic. We don't know how to get there. So we need women to lead us there.

Men are certainly capable of emotional vulnerability and commitment. But I don't believe most men will typically seek this kind of relationship. They must be led into it by women. They'll do it only if women demand that their own needs be met.

I keep advocating that women be empowered. Women have a special position in our culture where they can rein in some of this male behavior. When they do it, they gain. They win. They get more fulfillment. Because their needs are different than men's and they will at least infuse some stability in interpersonal relationships. And, thereby, into families. And then men's behavior will calm down. People will behave themselves a little bit better, resulting in a little more stability.

Adam: I think women have to realize that that thing they're attracted to in men is also where a lot of women get screwed. Here's the deal: A lot of women are attracted to this kind of Donald Trump behavior because the guy's a mover, a shaker, he's a captain of industry. Good is not good enough for Donald Trump. And that's what women are attracted to.

Now here's the downside to Donald Trump. Go ahead and get hooked up with him—he's still going to continue to do his thing. He didn't get where he is by saying to a woman "What do you need?" If he was that kind of guy who would say, "Oh, I'm going to stop now. I have a woman by my side," well, he would have done

ADAM's Personal Rating System, or PRS

Adam: This is something that goes on on a subconscious level every single day—but it's not really spoken about because people assume it makes them seem shallow.

Dr. Drew: It's a way people determine their initial attraction. It's not what makes relationships, it's not what makes passion.

Adam: We want to quantify people's attractiveness. It's not an attempt to figure out what's fair or what's just, what's right or what's wrong. This is what the opposite sex looks at when judging someone of the opposite gender.

Dr. Drew: The idea is that, whether we admit it or not, people who begin dating are rating each other—consciously or unconsciously—in a number of ways, all of them superficial. But if people could be honest about their own ratings—and then find people of a similar score to date—they would have a better chance of finding someone they could be compatible with.

Adam: You're doing best when you're dating someone whose score is a little bit higher.

Dr. Drew: What about the person who's a little higher? Does that mean they're not doing so good? Are they going to be disappointed or disillusioned in some way?

Adam: If they're grossly higher, they'll find out. I could go out with Cindy Crawford, but not for more than a month before she caught on. Because she's grossly higher. My only hope would be to somehow raise my score—like I replaced Jay Leno or they put the *Loveline* TV show on one of the major networks.

Dr. Drew: What makes people date lower than their score?

Adam: A combination of low self-esteem and control. I know plenty of guys who are a solid 7, 7.5, dating women no higher than a 4. Why? Because she's never going to cheat on him, she's never going to leave—she is going to do what he wants her to do.

Not that he's telling her to take out the garbage and polish the Porsche. Look at it this way: If you're a woman who is a little bit overweight, society is not banging down your door to get a date with you. If you're a guy who's in good shape, good-looking, with a little bit on the ball, and you're dating someone like this, who's the boss? Who's calling the shots? He is. He'd rather give up twenty pounds and take a little control. He knows she's not going to screw him over. She's going to be excited every time he comes over.

Dr. Drew: What about if it's the other way? If he's lower on the scale than she is?

Adam: There are guys who look at women almost the same way they look at a car. They want to be seen driving around in something nice to impress their peers, even if they can't really afford it. So they try to falsify their score to get the high-scoring girl, whether it's with a hairpiece or a fake Rolex.

Dr. Drew: It's pretty obvious what the guy is up to. What's going on with a woman who falls for that?

Adam: She buys the falsified number. She sees the fake Rolex and thinks, well, the guy's got money.

Dr. Drew: Here's a caveat in the PRS: You have to be honest with yourself about your rankings in every category. You can't overweigh the category. You need to do the evaluation honestly. Now, let's explain the categories.

Adam: There are four categories for guys to evaluate themselves:

Looks: Speaks for itself.

Personality: That pretty much speaks for itself. How the person functions at parties. Traditionally, people take personality almost as disposition, how they're going to treat their friends or their cat.

Sense of humor and intelligence: Give yourself up to 5 points for intelligence and up to 5 points for sense of humor.

Position: A person's position in life. Does a guy have a title, like CEO? Is he a doctor? An admiral?

Each category is worth 10 points. Guys should be honest when they rate themselves. You add up your total and divide by four—and that's your score.

Like, if you're an 8 in looks, a 5 in personality, a 7 in sense of humor and intelligence—but you clean carpets at night for a living, so you're a 2 in position. Your total is 22—which makes you a 5.5.

Dr. Drew: The categories are slightly different for women, aren't they?

Adam: Yeah. Here goes:

BODY: 10 points.

FACE: 10 points. (Hey, I know this sounds cruel, but these are the yardsticks guys use—and they definitely break women's looks into these two categories.)

PERSONALITY: It's who they are, what their beliefs are, what have you. It's not broken up like for men; intelligence and sense of humor are included in personality.

MANAGEABILITY: Ease of maintenance. How difficult are you? Would you let him go bowling with the guys?

Dr. Drew: It's the emotional health/security category.

Adam: Scoring is the same: Add up the total, divide by four, that's your score. But I also have two more litmus tests for how difficult a female is that ladies can try on themselves, and guys can use them, too.

FIRST: Ordering at a restaurant. Can you just look at a menu, point at what you want and order it without giving the waiter the third degree? A lot of women think they're putting together a bedroom set when they're ordering: "I want this, except I don't like asparagus, so can I take the au gratin potatoes from Number 14 and put it on this?" Like they're building a collage. Here's what you can do: You can go to a Thai place and tell them not to make it hot. That's as far as I'm willing to go with you. When you start inventing your own salad dressing, forget it.

SECOND: Pornography. Can you find a *Hustler* between the mattress and the box spring in your boyfriend's bedroom or on your husband's side of the bed and not spin out? Can you not look at this as cheating? Or can it just be your man giving himself some pleasure when you may not be available?

To me, those are both deal-breakers with a woman, no matter what her score.

it twenty years ago and he never would have had the power and you never would have gotten interested in him. A lot of women screw themselves by being attracted to the same thing that is going to kill them: "Now I'm involved with Donald Trump." And the guy's never home. Never home. He's not home with the kids, he's not home with you—he's in f-ing Taiwan making a deal on your anniversary.

2

Female Sexuality

Celebrity Input

★ ***from A. J. Dunning and Brian Vander Ark of The Verve Pipe***

★ ★ ★ **Q: Is it okay to use a vibrator? Do women like them? Should I worry that she'll like it better than me?**

Adam: Drew and I have done more talking about this subject than you or I ever thought we probably would. I do know that women enjoy this and you do run the risk of them, you know, taking it to the prom next year.

★ **A. J.:** Mom, Dad, I'd like you to meet Vibrator.

Dr. Drew: They just get dependent on it. And a woman who turns away from an emotional connection with a human to go for a mechanical object is somebody who's got some issues.

★ **Brian:** I think the key to all of this is that the man has actual possession of the vibrator. In other words, he keeps it locked in his gun safe, and then when he wants to bring it out and turn the woman on, then he does. Afterward, he puts it away in the gun safe.

Adam: Well, you treat it just like a loaded gun. You never leave the batteries in it when it's lying around. When you hand it to someone, you always hand them the handle end first, not the business end. It's always pointed down. It's always treated as if it has batteries in it.

Dr. Drew: Women can get desensitized from overuse. Just like guys that operate jackhammers can get numb hands, women can become sort of dependent on these vibrators. It's not thought to damage the nerves down there but it can desensitize a little bit. And you'd have to lay off for a while to cause things to come back or you might just become dependent on this machinery.

Adam: You're not going to be able to compete with it on a physical . . .

Dr. Drew: On a man-to-man basis. Man-to-machine.

Adam: You won't be able to compete.

Dr. Drew: The machine will win.

Adam: Women are lucky that there is no such invention for men because that would be the end of them. You'd really be shit out of luck. Because men *do* work that way. The day that somebody makes something that costs eight bucks and feels better than a woman, that's the day all dialogue is broken off.

Dr. Drew: Negotiations break down.

Adam: That's right. Thankfully women don't work that way. They usually need some emotional involvement. Guys may run a slight risk in introducing a vibrator to the sex play, but if the woman is healthy emotionally, then it can just be sort of an extension of her sexuality and it becomes an extra dimension, that helping hand, if you will, and another tool in your sexuality.

Q: Is it normal to masturbate?

Dr. Drew: Yes, of course. It's normal because humans almost have some sort of circuit where they naturally self-stimulate in lots of different ways. They do that when they're young children: They run around, spin themselves around, bang their heads, and do all kinds of self-stimulation. When people are coming out of a coma, men that is, the first thing they tend to do is start grabbing their penises. There is some natural connection there that occurs, and when people reach puberty, they begin to stimulate to the point of orgasm. It's normal. There's no reason for them not to; it's a way that people can master their functioning in a more reliable way.

Q: Do women do it, too?

Dr. Drew: Certainly although, typically, it isn't terribly interesting to them at a younger age. In this day and age, women are not discouraged from masturbating. The old notion that women are told not to is total BS. Women are not discouraged any more than young males are from touching their genitalia. You just tell them not to do it in public.

Adam: Women aren't discouraged against it, but I think there's still a societal thing that goes on where a woman is not comfortable talking about it.

Dr. Drew: They talk about it all the time among themselves, more than men do.

Adam: All right, but listen—if you have a man-ape, a sixteen-year-old male, and you have a sixteen-year-old female, and they both admit to masturbation, there's going to be a little more focus put on the woman, a little more fanfare around the woman's masturbation. Because guys are excited about it. Women would never ask a guy, "Do you masturbate?" so they could then go home and masturbate to the image of the guy masturbating. But a guy would, if a woman admitted to him that she masturbated.

Dr. Drew: Most women do not masturbate before the age of twenty or so. Some of it is developmental: Most women have not neuro-cognitively developed to

DR. DREW

on Estrogen: the Essence of Females

The hormone predominant in women is called estrogen. It's produced by the ovaries and stored in fat cells. It's also produced by the adrenal gland, particularly at the onset of puberty; even young males will produce a certain amount of estrogen.

Estrogen improves thinking cognition, stabilizes mood, and tends to protect against Alzheimer's disease, heart disease, and strokes. But an important role of estrogen in females is increasing receptivity to sexuality. It's believed that estrogen controls the desire to be penetrated, and ultimately causes the longing to have a baby.

Women also have a hormone called progesterone, produced by the ovaries and the adrenal glands. It has effects similar to the male hormone testosterone. It tends to put the brakes on a woman's receptiveness to sex. It can reduce libido,

understand what kind of feelings cause them to climax. It is not the same kind of masturbation, not the same kind of physical maneuver as it is for a man. It is not a purely physical maneuver.

Most of them don't figure out how to have an orgasm until they're well into their twenties, if ever. That's why many women do not experience orgasm during intercourse. Most of them need some kind of direct clitoral stimulation, oral stimulation usually. For them to masturbate, they also need that kind of emotional connection. They have to find that place in themselves, which is hard without another person. Many women have difficulty achieving that emotional state that allows them to masturbate, to explore orgasmic function.

So a twenty-year-old will often say, "I can't masturbate. I don't get it. It doesn't make sense." They can't quite figure it out.

Q: Why is the female orgasm so elusive?

Dr. Drew: It's different biology, totally different biology. It isn't compelling, isn't as necessary, and it is always, or usually, attached to an emotional state that women have to sort of figure out. For a man, it is purely a mechanical visual event that must occur with a certain regularity. With women, it's something that can occur or not, and it's much more connected to an emotional experience.

aggravate PMS, and decrease sensitivity to other hormones that influence sexual behavior. It can even decrease genital sensation and can cause irritability and depression, reducing the antidepressant nature of estrogen.

Celebrity Input

★ *from Actor Jon Cryer*

★ ★ ★ **Q: Why does my girlfriend talk about romance all the time. I buy her flowers once in a while. What more does she want?**

Dr. Drew: Women want to feel your emotional presence. She wants to feel it in a way that is assertive, dominant, not domineering but a real presence. It sweeps her off her feet in an emotional way. Just the way a guy wants to be swept away physically sometimes by a woman, women want that same presence on an emotional level. Although some men like to receive flowers, right, Jon?

★ **Jon:** I do. I'm a sucker for flowers because girls just don't think to give them.

Dr. Drew: That's interesting. It shows a real commitment from a woman to send you flowers.

★ **Jon:** I got some from my girlfriend very recently and it just bowled me over.

Dr. Drew: Adam has a theory, though, that flowers are just women screwing around with men because flowers have no purpose and they die in a couple of days and it's just doing something that's painful.

★ **Jon:** See, Adam is failing to look at flowers as a metaphor for life.

Adam: I think the thing with women and flowers—women want things to hurt a little bit. Women are looking for effort, even if it's just working real hard at your job to be able to afford flowers. They really look for effort. Guys are more bottom-line.

MYTHBUSTERS

Myth: *Women have their own form of ejaculation at the time of orgasm.*

The truth, according to Dr. Drew: In fact, some women will urinate at the time of orgasm. This is referred to as female orgasmic incontinence. Some women produce a great quantity of fluid, secreted from the various glands in and around the vagina and vulva, when properly stimulated. Though embarrassing to some women, it is part of normal functioning.

Dr. Drew: Men don't care how they got it just as long as they got it. Right?

Adam: Right. If a guy wanted a power drill or a circular saw for his birthday, he doesn't care how you get it for him. He doesn't care if you went shopping at Sears and Home Depot to get the lowest price or if you went next door and wrestled it away from the neighbor's kid who was hanging out in the garage with it. You could throw it at him two days early, unwrapped—and he'd be pleased as punch because he wanted that drill and now he's got it. He doesn't care if you made it yourself or if it fell off the truck in front of the house and you just scurried out in the street. He's got himself a new drill, that's the bottom line.

Women, they like a little suffering. They want to see that you went through a little work. This is why women love jewelry and flowers so much: because you've had to work hard to earn the money to buy them—and yet they know there is no practical value to them at all.

In a nuclear winter or some sort of major natural catastrophe, I don't care if that ring is two million dollars from Tiffany or ten dollars from Kmart, it's worth exactly the same. Which is nothing. On the other hand, if you put that money into a bunker in your front lawn or, you know, a Humvee or something like that, now you're in good shape.

Dr. Drew: You've got something, yeah.

Adam: Flowers are just a more extreme example. They're worthless, they're expensive, they die in three days. Men have their version—a thing like that that drives women crazy—with memorabilia like . . .

Dr. Drew: Baseball cards.

MYTHBUSTERS

Myth: *Women don't masturbate because they're taught not to.*

The truth, according to Dr. Drew: In reality, women are probably not discouraged any more significantly than men from touching their genitalia. It is more that the biology of the female is quite different. The mechanics of orgasmic function are more delicate, and much more intimately tied to the emotional experience in the female. Many women will describe feeling silly trying to masturbate because it doesn't accomplish anything; it doesn't necessarily even feel good because they haven't mastered a way to connect an emotional experience with the mechanical physical elements. In addition, the mechanical elements are substantially more complex than for the male. Many women do ultimately learn to masturbate, but this typically comes after adolescence.

ADAM on the Difference Between What Men and Women Find Sexy

Women have a sexual checklist, like men do. Except for men, the sexual checklists don't include other men. It does include anal sex and threesomes. It includes sex with your sister's best friend. But women have a little bit of a checklist, too, although anal sex and threesomes aren't necessarily high on their list. But for a lot of them, it's another woman, just to check it out.

Women are attracted to a guy's style, to his confidence and the way he carries himself. It's intangibles: confidence, success, talent—there's just something about him. It's attitude: They love confident guys. They'd rather have a less-attractive guy who's confident and secure than an Adonis who's nervous. It's the whole Clark Kent/Superman thing.

Women are like dogs or wolves, sensing fear in a man. That whole self-deprecating thing doesn't fly at all. Women aren't out there looking for a shopping buddy; they're looking for a leader. If they're wandering through the wilderness, they want a guy who says, "I know where to go—stick with me." They don't want wishy-washy guys; they want assertive, confident guys. They'll take homely guys if they're assertive and confident.

What turns guys on? It all boils down to getting women naked. For guys, it's ALL about tangibles—about looks and physicality. "I know she's short, she's flat-chested, and she's got a big ass—but there's just *something* about her." You *never* hear a guy say that.

For guys, there's nothing they like more than a beautiful woman who's not full of herself. That's the attraction of Elly May on *The Beverly Hillbillies:* She's a good-looking woman with a rope for a belt.

Men aren't looking for good qualities. They're looking for women who don't have bad qualities. Men look for women who won't: be a bitch, be a pain in the ass, complain when he goes out with his buddies. Men don't want a jigsaw puzzle; they want a clean slate. Women look for good qualities; they're proactive. Men are whatever the opposite of that is.

Adam: You're paying four thousand dollars for that football signed by Joe Namath and you aren't even going to play catch with it? Nope—just gonna stare at it. That's the same logic.

Q: What are women's major sexual fears and insecurities?

Dr. Drew: There's a lot of concern about normal sexual functioning. How their body looks. Most significantly, they're afraid the guy is not going to stay with them.

Adam: In terms of physicality, I would say women worry more about having a big ass than a small chest. A lot of women worry that they don't perform oral sex correctly. That's always something I try to put them at ease about because, really, how wrong can you go? As far as most guys are concerned, if she's doing it at all, she's doing it right. This is something that women conjured up on their own. It's not like there's a long history of men complaining about improper oral sex. I mean, there are, like, *no* documented cases of that.

Dr. Drew: They're extrapolating from how poorly it's done to them and how miserable that is.

Adam: Drew, that's why I've got the TV mounted on the ceiling at my place.

The thing that's ironic, I think—and this may sound sexist—but sexually, women don't have to perform too much. Men don't expect a ton out of them in the sack sexually. Men are really so thrilled that they're there at all; that's usually enough. I've slept with a few women in my day and some were better than others—but I never ran into one where I thought, *Oh, this is miserable. This is like pulling teeth. This is horrible.* Sure, sometimes it's not a great match, but you're still getting there, breaking a sweat. It's still pizza, as we would say, and pizza is always good, no matter what. Women do not have to perform, yet they put more pressure on themselves to perform—where men put almost no pressure on themselves to perform.

Dr. Drew: That's not true. That's what makes their penises fail them.

Adam: Okay, not all men. Look, if you liken sex to football, the guy would be more of a quarterback, a running back—and the girl would be more of a guard or a tackle. She's got to suit up, she's got to get out there—but the game isn't hinging on her. She's not going to win or lose the game; she just has to be there. Men don't put enough pressure on themselves to perform, while women put too much pressure on themselves. Although Drew's right, there are a percentage of guys who put way too much pressure on themselves and then can't rise to the occasion.

Q: What about women who are insecure because of their inability to achieve orgasm?

Dr. Drew: Common. Here's the deal people don't understand. We've said this before, but women often aren't neuro-cognitively developed at a young age to understand what kind of feelings cause them to climax. It's not the same kind of physical maneuver that it is for a man. It is not a purely physical maneuver. Most of them don't figure out how to have an orgasm until they're well into their twenties, if ever. And most of them don't have an orgasm during intercourse; they have it during oral sex or some secondary form of stimulation.

Adam: If genitalia were languages, the vagina would be Japanese, or Finnish. The penis would be like pig Latin, or pidgin English. Very little to work out; nothing you couldn't learn in a weekend, especially with the folks out of town.

Women really have to put in the time. Some of them get a little frustrated early and that's it. They kind of sign off.

Dr. Drew: But it's such an emotional event for them that they usually have to figure out the space and the feelings for functioning to proceed. They can't just hope the mechanics will work themselves out.

Q: Why is sex initially unsatisfying for young women?

Dr. Drew: For most people, the first time is not very gratifying. I mean, who has a good experience the first time? Nobody.

Adam: No one I've ever met.

Q: Can men tell if a woman is faking an orgasm?

Adam: No.

Dr. Drew: You should feel the muscular contraction in her vagina. But in the heat of things, you might not feel that anyway. And women can fake that, too.

Adam: It's like saying, "Can you tell when an actress is faking crying?" Well, the tears are coming out—is she faking? No, she's thinking about her dead grandpa, but it's really Al Pacino telling her about something else and they're hoping they're still able to evoke the feeling and manufacture it. I would say probably a good half of faked orgasms have some pleasure involved.

But no, a guy's not going to know—and a guy's not going to care, as a matter of fact. A guy is believing what he wants to believe when it comes to a woman's gratification. He certainly is not going to question the gift.

Q: Should she ever need to fake an orgasm?

Adam: I don't think she should have to, but there's certainly a place for it. This is like saying, should you have to lie when a woman asks you, "Do I look fat?"

You could tell them to turn around. You could get out some sort of caliper, do a water displacement test. But in reality, what you say is, "No. Now let's go eat." There are certain times when that's all right. But a lot of women think guys are going to be offended if they knew an orgasm was faked. When, in fact, this is the greatest gift for a man.

Dr. Drew: Here's the difference between Adam and Drew, right here.

Adam: Listen guys, let's not discourage this, because they just may go away altogether. I really have this approach to life, a little naive perhaps, but there's just a lot of stuff that I don't want to know. There really is. You know, 85 percent of life is perception. It's like, hey, you're enjoying that hot dog at the ball game—let's not focus on the slaughterhouse where it came from. Because you'll spit that damn thing right out.

You can take that part of life to an extreme and never leave the house. I'm not saying you should install a theme park in your skull and just sort of live life that way. If someone says, "Hey, you look good," just take it and don't try to figure out whether they're lying or not. "Hey, you had an orgasm? Great!"

★ from Comic Caroline Rhea

★ ★ ★ **Q: Whenever I go to perform oral sex on my girlfriend, I get grossed out by the smell. But how do I tell her she stinks?**

★ **Caroline:** If you feel that way, then you don't love women entirely. And it's so disgusting to objectify her into parts. You either love the woman that you are with and you want to please her or you don't. Men who don't want to perform oral sex, it's like: Get lost, forever and ever. Sorry, that's my opinion.

Dr. Drew: No, that's a good answer. I think, Caroline, since I last saw you, I've gotten more and more militant about my message of empowering women. Interpersonally, I'm just so sick of women thinking their role in a relationship is to please a man and men thinking that's the role of women, too. It creates instability and leaves women to believe they should behave like men. In fact, they should rely on their unique instincts as a female human being, which leads to much healthier relationships and much greater intimacies.

Adam: If you tell her she stinks, she's gonna be offended—obviously. The best plan is to come from a place of concern for her health. You explain that you were either watching the *Loveline* show on TV or listening to it on the radio and you heard a young woman call up and talk about this very problem. And Drew explained that it's often caused by an infection or something that's gone terribly wrong down there, that it's a health risk, and this is how it manifests itself. And that he urged this caller to get checked out by the doctor for fear there may be a health problem. So you just explain that you heard Drew saying that, that you noticed a little something and were concerned about her health.

DR. DREW on the Difference Between STDs and Gynecological Problems

How can you tell the difference between a sexually transmitted disease and a gynecological problem?

Really, you can't.

The signs of an STD are typically vaginal irritation, pain with intercourse, discharge, ulcers, or any painful lesions about the vagina or vulva. But these are very nonspecific symptoms; vaginitis, which is an infection of the vagina, can cause similar symptoms.

Here's a quick rundown of a couple of the most common gynecological problems and their symptoms:

Vaginitis is an infection that is easily treatable; symptoms include vaginal irritation, pain with intercourse, and discharge. It's potentially sexually transmitted and can be transmitted back and forth. It causes no disease in men, although men can transmit it to women. Women usually can treat it very simply with a vaginal cream.

A **yeast infection** is a kind of vaginitis. Symptoms include a whitish discharge, with a lot of itching and irritation. Women can get over-the-counter yeast preparations like Gyne-Lotrimin and Monistat. If they aren't better in two or three days, they have something else going on.

Symptoms of a **bladder infection** include pain with urination, pain over the pubic bone and in the back, fever, weakness, and fatigue. If left untreated, it can move into the kidneys, causing a much more serious and potentially life-threatening kidney infection. It's usually treated with antibiotics.

In general, women should not make an assumption about what it is they've got going on, because the symptoms are so similar that there's no way for them to tell by themselves. To be safe, they should see their doctor.

3

Male Sexuality

Too much time on a man's hands equals too much time with his penis in his hands.
—ADAM CAROLLA

(We thought it would be interesting to include the questions we might have asked when we were younger and going through these kinds of things. Here's the first set; there are more throughout the book.)

Young Drew: *Hi, I'm thirteen. I was at a school dance and there was a girl there who my friends tell me wanted to dance with me. I was so scared to ask her to dance, I really don't think she wanted to dance with me.*

Adam: *Do you trust your friends?*

Young Drew: *These were friends of hers that told me this. But I felt so funny when I was trying to, I don't know, it was so confusing to me. I couldn't do it. I was* *just paralyzed. Since then, my friends have been bugging me why I didn't do it. I told them I didn't like her.*

Adam: *Did you have interest in her?*

Young Drew: *Yeah, I did, I really do.*

Adam: *But you were afraid that, if you went over to her, the friends would all have known what was going on, and now you'd be forced to sort of come through?*

Young Drew: *Yeah. I just felt so overwhelmed I just didn't know what to do and so I couldn't. I felt too funny.*

Dr. Drew: *It's normal to be awkward about these kinds of things. Do you have any other experience asking a girl out or going up to somebody?*

Young Drew: *No, I just can't do that. Nothing makes me feel worse.*

Dr. Drew: *At your age, that's not uncommon. It's a skill you're going to have to learn. The sooner you get on with it, the more skilled you're going to be at this. Relationships at your age can be very intense but they're not going to be lifetime commitments. It's awkward at your age to try to relate to a girl when you don't even know who you are yourself; it's normal to feel this way.*

You've got to understand that humans develop, mature, and emotionally evolve only by virtue of connections with other people. At your age, there's opportunity for growth because each connection is a new one; it's an opportunity for new interactions, for learning new things about yourself. And if you don't have those opportunities you stay stagnant, you don't know who you are or develop a sense of self.

Young Drew: *You haven't told me what I should do with this girl. Should I continue to pursue it? I sort of think I'll just drop it.*

Adam: *She knows you kind of turned her down at the dance, you didn't go up and talk to her, right?*

Young Drew: *No, I feel silly, I feel like an idiot.*

Adam: *But she likes you, you know that.*

Young Drew: *Maybe not anymore, though.*

Adam: *I think you ought to go back and talk to her. I think you ought to just be straight up with her.*

Q: What is most guys' biggest sexual fear?

Adam: Not getting enough of it. We do deal with people who have dysfunction, premature ejaculation. But I would say not getting any is the biggest fear.

Dr. Drew: That and penis size.

Adam: I think for a lot of guys it's plain old getting laid. You could take all the guys with questions about function and size and all that and it wouldn't amount to as many guys who are worried about not getting it.

Young Adam: *I'm seventeen and live in North Hollywood, and I can't seem to get a second date. Matter of fact, I can barely get a first date with girls I want to go out with.*

Dr. Drew: *Do you have a girlfriend?*

Young Adam: *No. You kidding?*

Dr. Drew: *Have you ever dated a girl steadily?*

Young Adam: *Not since the seventh grade.*

Dr. Drew: *I'm not clear what's really bothering you.*

Young Adam: *I just want to know how to get some dates, how to get more confidence. Women don't like me at all.*

Dr. Drew: *It's so normal for someone your age to feel like that. You're only seventeen; you have a lot of time to build your confidence. Particularly at that age, young men have no sense of who they are because they have nothing to present. That's why women tend to go out with older guys.*

Adult Adam: *I think that's true. Men don't have any sense of who they are at that age. Women seem to lose their sense of who they are as they get older, but women got it all together as seniors in high school.*

Young Adam: *I think I'm my own worst enemy. I don't feel good about myself. I don't feel attractive, I don't feel desirable. I'm desperate. I come across like a death-row inmate.*

Dr. Drew: *Women pick up on that, especially at that age. They're feeling in-*

complete, too, and if they have another incomplete person on their hands, they can't handle that.

Adult Adam: *This is an age-old problem and there's really no fast track here. What you need to do is, when you find a girl you'd like to ask out, you need to sort of close your eyes and realize that this is all going to pass very quickly. If she tells you to go f— off, it's just going to be another funny story for you to tell your kids about one day when you're married to the woman you love.*

Dr. Drew: *Something you know a lot about.*

Adult Adam: *I've seen pictures. This is not going to make or break you. Stop treating it like it is.*

Young Adam: *It feels like it will.*

Dr. Drew: *It feels like the end of the world, like no one has really gone through it before.*

Adult Adam: *And the reason it feels like it is going to make or break you is: You are so precariously perched right now that anything is going to send you tumbling.*

Dr. Drew: *And you're looking for life preservers.*

Q: I think my penis is too small. What should I do?

Adam: Most guys don't realize that the average penis is smaller than they think. Most guys assume the average size is six inches. That figure has been bandied about for years. But the reality is, like, 5.1 or 5.2 inches erect. I figure it's a lot of Asian researchers came up with that figure. The bottom line is, whoever is in charge of the research is probably 5.3; therefore, the average size is 5.2. Whatever—it's smaller than people think.

As a matter of fact, when guys think they've got a problem—a small penis—and we tell them the average is 5.2 inches, they're so relieved. All of a sudden, they're big again.

Dr. Drew: But they don't really feel any better. So we have to get at what's really troubling them.

It also helps if we have a woman confirm that women are not particularly concerned with size, that this is a male issue. Men are concerned with size; women aren't, except at extreme ends of the curve. And the one that surfaces most in discussions with women is not the penis that's too small but the one that's too big.

Q: Why are guys so worried about the size of their penises?

Adam: I would say the size thing has climbed in the last five years in our society. There used to be more ballyhoo about it, more jokes and stuff, things about hand size, blah blah blah. Women have done a pretty good job of dispelling this and sort of putting it in reality. It was always speculation about what women want: "Chicks dig this. . . . No, this is what they like."

In the last ten years, the Madonnas of the world have said, "Listen, guys, here's what women want," and one of them was that they didn't care about size. And a collective sigh of relief was heard from the male population.

Dr. Drew: Ultimately, if they're worried about not getting any, it's "My penis is small, therefore I won't get any." The penis is a symbol of self-worth.

I'm amazed how much the size thing does come up. And it always comes up with guys who have other issues about their self-worth. I think there is some biological evolutionary precedent for the notion that men's physical size, both stature and penis size, has some sort of biological advantage. There's some primitive remnant of territorial biology operating there.

We usually slip right past that and get at what's really troubling the guy. A lot of the time, it's either that they're someone who has significant psychological or social issues. Or else they're twelve and worried about being normal. They wonder if they'll be okay when a girl sees it.

Adam: It's kind of funny. It's really the only part on a male's body that he ever questions: Is it going to grow any more?

A boy, at age fourteen, doesn't look at his calves or his ears or his nose and question whether it's going to grow any more; he just assumes that, as he grows, it

ADAM explains: Why Do Guys Buy Penis Enlargers?

A penis enlarger is to guys what a slimming device is to women: It's like the ultimate infomercial. It's a lucky thing they can't put these things on TV. If you did a half-hour infomercial for penis enlargers, they'd outsell any piece of workout equipment ever. Because guys want to believe.

Guys would like to have a big penis like women would love to have a great ass and thighs. But ab-buster devices are as ridiculous as penis enlargers.

Most guys take this angle: For $29.95, if it only feels good, it's worth the postage and handling. How much of a downside can there be? Even if it took a quarter-inch off, they'd still use it.

Do they work? Of course not. It's like saying you can make your nose bigger by smashing it with a rolling pin. If you put a suction device on your finger, you're going to get some will grow, too. They don't single out their shoulder or their knees and say, "I'm worried that it's stopped growing."

But the penis—there's always a question. "Gee, it hasn't budged in a week. No noticeable growth in girth or length in the last three to five days and I'm worried sick about it." This is what young guys worry about. They ought to worry about their IQ size, because it's usually the same size.

Most often, they're also the guys who objectify women totally. What happens is their penis has become their tool and the woman is just sort of a project that they're working on with their tool. If they've got a little brad-nailer instead of a sledgehammer, they don't think they're going to get the job done. These aren't the guys who are worried about their ability to cuddle. . . .

Dr. Drew: . . . or to have a relationship.

Q: If I buy one of those penis pumps, will it make my penis larger? Could my penis explode?

Dr. Drew: No, it won't explode. It also won't get any larger. The reason we know that is because they cost $39, not $3,900.

Adam: That's always been my point. The day someone makes one of these things that works, it will cost $3,900. Not the same price as a toaster oven. Believe you me. Anything that makes your penis larger, it's got to cost at least four grand. That's it.

Q: When should I start worrying about impotency or premature ejaculation?

Adam: Men don't worry about the premature-E or not getting it up unless they're experiencing it. It's like worrying about prostate cancer: "Listen, as long as I'm pissing twice a day and it's going good, I'll cross that bridge when I get to it." That's how guys are.

Q: I have never had sex with an uncircumcised man before. Is there anything different I need to know about satisfying him?

Dr. Drew: No. You need to know that this is one of the only countries on Earth where circumcised men are more common than uncircumcised men. Put it this way: It looks a little different, but it's the same instrument.

Adam: Right. It's really the difference between, like, an alto and a tenor sax, or a—what's the one that Kenny G plays? It looks like a goddam oboe or something. You know what I'm talking about? It's the gayest-looking instrument.

Dr. Drew: What are you saying: that uncircumcised penises look gay?

Adam: No. But here's the other thing. Saying, "I've never been with an uncircumcised man" is a little like saying, "Should I know anything about a Hispanic man before I'm with him?" It's just a person, right?

Q: I have a bunch of little white bumps on the side of my penis. They don't hurt, they don't change, they don't do anything. What can I do about them?

Dr. Drew: These are probably the pearly penile papules, which appear around puberty. They are little white bumps. They are usually symmetrical and

swelling. I'm sure you can aggravate or inflame your penis to increase the circumference, but it will probably have to be drained by a surgeon.

As for these guys who put weights on their penis and stretch it out over the years, that's like taking the best chili a guy ever made and saying, "Well, if you put a bottle of ketchup in it, it will go further." How far can you stretch it before it doesn't work? What good is it if your penis is a half-inch longer but it's covered with scar tissue?

Give me a small working penis over a big one that doesn't work. On myself, that is. I'm not soliciting.

they are usually around the base. If you're not sexually active, that's really all it could be. If you are concerned, have a doctor look at it. If you are sexually active, warts can look somewhat like this and ought to be checked out.

Q: My girlfriend noticed that I have two different-sized testicles. Should I be embarrassed? What can I do to even them out?

Adam: That's just the way it is, sometimes. There are just guys with one small one and one big one. There should be some sort of donor program where you can match yourself up. But there'd be a lot longer line in the big testicle department: If I have one small one and one big one, and you have one small one, one big one, who's getting two small ones?

Dr. Drew: The fact is it's common to have asymmetry of size and position. Usually that is caused by enlargement of the epididymis, sort of a cap on top of the testicle. It's the sperm-processing center. There can be cysts that are just fluid-filled bodies, and those sometimes need to be taken out. They can sometimes affect function and fertility. Hernias can appear like an extra or larger testicle, so it's something that should be checked out by a doctor, particularly if any part of the enlargement is hard, like a rock or pebble. That can be a tumor and needs to be checked out. And if they are enlarging rapidly, that's another reason to see a doctor quickly.

★ ***from Comic Marlon Wayans***

Q: I have a penis with a big curve to the right. Is this normal?

★ **Marlon:** It would be great if you are trying to catch a cab or if you hitchhike. Otherwise, I don't know, I guess you've got to find a woman that curves to the right as well.

Adam: Another Republican. Here's what I know about this. Unless there is pain involved, don't do anything about it. Because the procedure that straightens it out shortens it, as well. When we talk to people about it, all you have to do is mention that the procedure shortens the penis and they are suddenly able to go on living with it. Immediately. As a matter of fact, if you talk about anything, any problem, no matter what it is, and the answer is your penis gets shortened, to correct it—

★ **Marlon:** —guys are not going to do it.

Adam: They move on.

Dr. Drew: Really, it becomes abnormal only at the point of pain or dysfunction. Otherwise, it's more a question of function and comfort. If there is no function problem, no symptoms, then it's normal.

★ **Marlon:** You just make sure that, when you have sex with her, you make sure you position her in a way that you don't rupture an ovary or something.

Adam: Right. You don't want to poke it out of her side. But seriously, you know what a lot of guys don't know is that most guys have a little bit of English down there.

Q: Is it normal for a guy to be insecure about his sexual performance?

Dr. Drew: Here's something we don't really acknowledge in the culture—and that is that our sexuality is a big part of ourselves. That's who we are and how we experience ourselves. And most of us are pretty insecure about that, particularly as it pertains to our relations to others, which is what sex is. So it's natural enough that we should have insecurities there.

Women are less insecure. They want to make sure the guy is happy—that kind of thing. But guys are really concerned about it. Their identity is wrapped up in being able to adequately perform.

Adam: Well, it's like this. A man and a woman go out to play a game of miniature golf. If the woman loses, she doesn't care. If the guy loses, he's pissed and the evening is ruined.

ADAM on Why Male Masturbation Is Not a Substitute for Sex

Basically, here's the misnomer in society: that masturbation is what you do when you can't have sex.

"Oh, look at him. He can't get none, so he's pulling his pud"—and all that kind of stuff.

And that's basically how it starts off when you're in junior high. But the reality is, as you get older, for most guys it becomes its own little entity. It's not sex, it's not intercourse, it's not a substitute for sex, it's not this, it's not that—it's just what it is, masturbation.

For many guys, this has been the only thing that stuck by them through the tough times. Friends come and go, nations crumble—but this has been something that never betrayed you. The hand never cheated on you—it doesn't even look at other penises. You know what I'm saying.

Dr. Drew: That's the point, I think. The way we develop as human beings, our sexuality is an extremely important part.

Adam: Anything that's physical, that has to do with someone else, immediately turns into competition. It's kind of weird, but if you take two people and you put them together—on the basketball court or on a bowling lane or a tennis court—if there's sweat involved, there's some kind of competition.

People want to achieve and they want to do well. This one hits at the core. If someone is no good at bowling, it doesn't really destroy his ego. But sex—that's something that's all-encompassing.

Dr. Drew: Yeah, it's self-worth.

Q: Is it possible to masturbate too much?

Dr. Drew: Yes, if it affects one's productivity.

Adam: There's excessive anything.

Dr. Drew: If they hurt themselves. If they can't function, if they can't have meaningful relationships, if it affects their schoolwork. That's excessive.

Adam: I think a lot of times, it becomes like this aggressive act for a lot of men; they work out a lot of hostility and anger. It sounds comical but it's true.

Say a guy breaks up with a girl. He's grief-stricken, angry, vindictive, potentially a few beers away from causing some trouble. So he's staying home and having these aggressive fantasies about her and masturbating five times a day. It's not healthy, but it's benign.

Dr. Drew: It's better than the alternatives.

Adam: I definitely think too much masturbation is a sign of unhealthiness. But no masturbation at all is a sign of unhealthiness. I think it's one of those things where, if you feel sort of comfortable with yourself, then you do it when you feel like it and you don't when you don't feel like it.

And then a woman comes in after you've got a good ten years under the belt, or just beneath the belt, with this kind of activity, and she'd really like to wean the man away from himself. It's the same as saying, "Your dad got you this dog right before he died. Now you're hooked up in this relationship with me and I'd like you to leave the dog alone."

It's really the litmus test with women. A woman is secure if she can walk in and see a guy with a *Playboy* (or whatever) spread out, taking care of business and A) either be turned on by it, or B) be ambivalent about it. And I say ambivalent in the sense of not really caring.

Q: What's the weekly masturbating average for a guy?

Dr. Drew: The average ends up being a couple of times a week, I would say.

Adam: For one guy? Maybe for you. You're used to having dorm mates or something. A couple of times a week would fall way under the North Hollywood curve. My friends growing up were good for, I would say, minimum once a day. There were plenty of days in there where they had multidays. My friends were good for, on average, I would say, ten times a week. Most of them were still up there, once or twice a day, ten years later.

Dr. Drew: There was a survey two years ago about human sexual behavior that said the average married couple was having sex about 1.5 times a week. And masturbation came near that.

Adam: I really think sex with a partner and masturbation are two different entities that sort of end up at the same place. Same outcome. It's like, at the ball game, you got the peanut guy and the hot dog guy. They're both at the ball game, they're both selling stuff to eat, they're both making a buck, they're both shouting out—but it's a different thing. Women make the mistake of thinking of masturbation as a substitute for sex.

Celebrity Input ★ from Comic Caroline Rhea

Q: I'm a twenty-two-year-old guy and I find that I want to masturbate whenever I'm alone. Can I hurt myself doing this?

Adam: Of course you jack off whenever you're alone. That's when it goes down.

★ **Caroline:** What are you using that's going to hurt so much?

Adam: I guess if you really got going, to the point where the bed was vibrating enough that it shook the bookshelf adjacent to it and a bowling trophy worked its way off and you were impaled on it.

Dr. Drew: Here's the deal, if you are physically in pain, you are hurting yourself. Or if you are doing this so much that it pulls you away from other productive—

★ **Caroline:** Pardon the pun there.

Dr. Drew: —other productive parts of your life or relationships, then it's a problem.

★ **Caroline:** And you know when else it's a problem? If you are the President. That would be the other time that it would be a problem.

Dr. Drew: It turns out people who are excessively preoccupied with this sometimes become

ADAM says: You Know You're Masturbating Too Much When . . .

- It hurts to straighten your fingers.
- The Kleenex Corporation considers your purchase of their stock as a cash-back rebate.
- The local sperm bank offers you health benefits and a 401k plan.
- Your boss insists that you clock out before you go to the bathroom.
- You realize that the width of your dick is mostly a callus.
- Your mom has to snap your tube sock over her knee like kindling to get it into the washer.

that way from sexual abuse. People who really are sort of bizarrely preoccupied. So if it's impairing your relationships, it's a problem.

★ **Caroline:** How about this: If somebody is masturbating all the time, then reality is no longer reality. If they are always thinking about porn or whatever they are masturbating to, then the person you are with doesn't really have a chance. Because they are actually three-dimensional—in some cases, four.

Dr. Drew: A lot of that behavior is a way to avoid intimacy. It's a way to avoid feelings and intimacy. Of course you are going to be more involved with that than with a person. While relating to a person offers the richness of the connection, there is also the risk of getting hurt. Some people desperately want to avoid that.

Adam: I have pushed the envelope on this particular subject as a youth and I've never been put in harm's way because of it. Actually I did get a calf cramp once. But no, what can happen is you can sort of lose a little zest for life. I believe a man needs a little fuel in the tank to get him through the day. It is a motivator. And sometimes when you are in the constant state of depletion, you're not really motivated. When you eliminate women from the mix, you also eliminate a lot of other things. Like, your career aspirations go out the window, too, because half the reasons guys make money is just to get a nice car so they can find nice women and have sex. It's almost like a bong-load, jacking off. It's not going to kill you, but do it too much and you don't tend to get much else done.

- It takes two people and a crowbar to pry open your sister's Victoria's Secret catalog.
- You're diagnosed with carpal tunnel syndrome even though you've been unemployed for the past year.
- Plunging the toilet feels like déjà vu.
- If instead of a squirt, it makes a puff, and you wind up dusting your belly instead of mopping it.
- You couldn't make it through this list without squeezing one off.

DR. DREW on Testosterone: What Makes a Guy a Guy

Testosterone is a hormone produced by the testes under the influence of the brain. Enlarged doses tend to elevate your mood. It also determines masculine characteristics, such as beard, body hair, musculature. Testosterone produces and maintains sperm. Increases in testosterone lead to increases in sexual thoughts, fantasies, and desire.

Testosterone also influences a man's assertiveness, aggressiveness, and self-confidence. Guys with high levels of testosterone tend to be independent; it makes them strive to be separate in ways that women can't comprehend, even though women have a low level of testosterone as well. Testosterone levels tend to go up with increased sexual activity and stimulation. They also go up when men achieve levels of success and leadership.

You show me a guy who jacks off eight to ten times a day, and I'll show you a guy who's not living the dream. We were trying to do a little math yesterday. I've got seventeen years under my belt.

Dr. Drew: That's three hundred sixty-five times seventeen. That's about five thousand. Well, with a few good days in there—maybe seven thousand?

Some Penis Facts

- Average penis length (flaccid): 3.5 inches
- Average penis length (erect): 5.1 inches
- Average percent increase in volume, flaccid to erect: 300
- Average number of erections per night while sleeping: 5
- Average duration of each nocturnal erection: 20–30 minutes
- Average time to ejaculation during intercourse: 2 minutes
- Average body's sperm production: 50,000 per minute; 72 million per day
- Average number of sperm in ejaculation of average fertile man: 200–600 million
- Average volume of semen in ejaculation: 0.5–1 teaspoon
- Percentage of sperm in ejaculation: 3
- Average number of ejaculatory spurts: 3–10

4

Virginity and Becoming Sexually Active

Q: My girlfriend and I are both virgins and are both nervous about the first time. I'm afraid it will happen too fast and she won't dig me anymore. Any suggestions?

Dr. Drew: It will happen too fast—and she probably won't enjoy it. It's just the way it is the first time. And women basically do it to satisfy the man anyway. Very few of them have a great experience the first time out.

Adam: The first time out of the chute, probably not.

Dr. Drew: Many women end up with a fantasy that the first guy is going to be their one and only. That's very rare.

Adam: But doing anything before you want to do it, whether it's sex or getting up in the morning, is painful.

Q: Does losing your virginity cause physical changes?

Dr. Drew: Very often in women, there can be a hymen that ruptures, which is a membrane just inside the vagina. That can be uncomfortable and can cause a bit of bleeding. Beyond that, there isn't any substantial physical change. A lot of women have a preoccupation that it's going to stretch them or change them. People have to remember that this is a birth canal, something that was designed to accommodate a baby's head and spring back quite nicely.

Adam: A guy's physical metamorphosis—

Dr. Drew: —occurs in the brain.

Adam: In a guy, the chest expands, the chin tends to protrude. The shoulders get pulled back. Oftentimes, the right hand can swell up from a lot of high-fiving with a male counterpart.

Q: Does losing your virginity cause psychological changes?

Dr. Drew: For women, clearly there's a biological basis for the intensity of feelings for the other person. There are elevated levels of serotonin and endorphins, so people's moods can be better. None of these are exclusively associated with virginity. It's just getting to the point of intercourse for any couple.

Adam: Symbolically, you become a man, if you think about it.

Dr. Drew: You cross the threshold to something.

Adam: Yeah—and with women, in a certain sense you enter the adult world.

Dr. Drew: Certainly biologically, you're into the realm of procreation. That has a responsibility and a whole set of behaviors and reality attached to it.

Adam: Physically, it's no big deal. Emotionally, because of the buildup society has put to it, symbolically it means something.

Q: Should it be a big deal?

Adam: It shouldn't be a big deal for guys.

Dr. Drew: It needn't be as big a deal for guys. But it acknowledges a certain level of responsibility, a certain level of commitment and involvement with another person that you have to be prepared for emotionally and developmentally. So, yeah, it should be a big deal because it bonds you in a way that you may not be ready for.

Should it be an absolute taboo prior to marriage? I think we both say no to that. It's better to have a physical relationship before marriage and find out what each other is all about. To explore the depth of the relationships before you make a lifelong commitment.

Adam: Right. Put it this way: If you're in too big a hurry to get rid of your virginity, or if you cling to it too much—

Dr. Drew: —there's a problem. It's always suspect when one or the other is going on. But there's a reason for that.

Adam: When I was a virgin, I was thinking about not being a virgin and getting it over with. I wasn't really thinking about falling in love. I wasn't even thinking about enjoying it. I was looking at it more like an Army physical. I just wanted to find out I didn't have a clubfoot, and get on with my life.

Dr. Drew: You also feel like you're crawling into a world where sex will continue. It wouldn't end with just a single episode. It was like you had crossed over into new territory.

Adam: We put so much weight on it as a society that you actually think there is going to be some sort of magical power that comes along with it. Before I had a girlfriend, before I was in a relationship, I used to think to myself, *If I had a good woman and I had sex every night, I could probably go out and conquer the business world, too. She'd make me feel like a king.* When I was doing stand-up, if I got a blow job that afternoon, I would be so confident onstage that night. In fact, I was probably an ounce and a half lighter and other than that, there wasn't any significant difference.

You find that things don't change. I thought that, after I lost my virginity, *that* was going to be *it.*

Dr. Drew: You were going to be hanging with Hef and James Caan in the grotto at the Playboy Mansion from that moment on.

Adam: Right—starting that evening. As it turns out, I had a two-year layoff before I got laid again and it didn't really change a thing.

Q: How do I deal with the social pressure—both to keep it and to lose it?

Adam: It's hard. We still put so much behind it. With women, we tend to think biblically, in terms of societal mores and that kind of thing. With guys, I think there's a lot behind it as well, although it's not quite as clear as it is with women.

With women, society's message is fairly cut and dried: If you're a virgin, you're pure and clean. If you're not, look out—oh, boy, aren't your parents going to be disappointed!

But as guys, there's a lot of significance to it as well. I would almost say that, for a guy who's eighteen or nineteen or twenty who's still a virgin, he's probably having a rougher go of it than a woman who is that age and a virgin. Or, if you want to go the other way, I'd say a fifteen- or sixteen-year-old girl who isn't a virgin is probably not getting as hard a time as a nineteen-year-old male who is.

Q: Can you wait too long to lose your virginity?

Dr. Drew: I think we've found that, when people are virgins later into their life, twenty-five or beyond, it's usually because something is really up with them. I suspect the same is true for guys who have to have the woman be a virgin. They're going to have problems with a woman who is sexually active.

Adam: Well, here's the situation: There is a very small percentage of society, males and females, whose religion dictates that they stay virgins, who are very devout and that's what they're basing their sexuality on. I believe they're a little screwed up, too, but let's just say for 2 or 3 percent of society who are hard-core Catholics, this is a serious issue and they're going to stand by that. For the rest of society, the people who are virgins too late into life usually have some other issues.

Show me a twenty-four-year-old virgin—even show me a twenty-one-year-old virgin—and I'll show you someone who's a little bit off, someone who has some issues. Absolutely. You show me a twenty-two-year-old guy who needs to be with someone who's a virgin, I'll show you some more issues. It's sort of like, the more stock either sex puts into it, usually the more issues surround that individual. Whether it's that they need someone else to be a virgin or it's "I'm going to be a virgin," there are usually some issues that go along with it.

Q: Are there other problems with waiting?

Dr. Drew: People frequently feel anxious and less worthwhile because they've fallen behind their peers. Initially, they may have fallen behind intentionally because they were trying to restrain themselves. But they start feeling bad about it.

Adam: For a guy, it starts screwing with your confidence. You feel somewhat stigmatized.

Dr. Drew: Women say the same thing. For women, it's that their girlfriends are wanting them to join them. They feel a little jealous and start pulling peers into their world.

Q: How long should you wait?

Adam: Realistically, I would say eighteen is a nice number for a woman. I think anybody in this day and age whose daughter made it until her eighteenth birthday, hymen intact, should consider themselves pretty successful.

Dr. Drew: For a woman, before that age, they're not developed to be able to manage those feelings without being quite traumatized. I'd agree with Adam that eighteen is a safe, healthy age.

Q: And for guys?

Adam: Since it's more of a thing of getting it out of the way, rather than an emotional thing, you pick it: fifteen, whatever. It's almost like: Okay, check it off the list.

It might even be better for society if, whenever a guy turned fifteen, the state took him to a brothel and got him laid. Sort of got it out of the way for him. Then he could relax and see about getting into a relationship.

Q: What about losing it at younger ages?

Dr. Drew: Guys want to have sex before the age of sixteen but, typically, can't.

Adam: Because the girls won't let them.

Dr. Drew: Right. So we don't really talk to too many of them. And the girls who are having sex before the age of sixteen, they're immediately suspect. There's typically something going on.

The scientific data is that the neuro-cognitive adaptation is not evolved to the point that girls would be able to manage the intense feelings associated with physical intimacy; that's just the scientific reality. For them to have sex is usually acting out—something is developmentally awry.

Q: I'm a fourteen-year-old girl and when my boyfriend and I try to have sex, it's really painful. What can we do?

Dr. Drew: A fourteen-year-old having sex: It's unpleasant, it's your body telling you something. I say you probably shouldn't be doing this. You're anxious. The most common reason for this is spasms of the floor of the pelvic muscles. And certainly plenty of lubricant will help with this, but it doesn't change the fact that your body is telling you that you're anxious and you're not ready. Do you agree?

Adam: There is a bottom line, which is: It's not working out. It can be emotional or it could be physiological or it could be both. It's probably something emotional that manifests itself and becomes physiological. And either way, it's a fairly clear message. Which is that you should give it another couple of years. You're growing up too fast.

Q: Are there other reasons that it's harder for women at younger ages?

Dr. Drew: Typically, women fantasize that the first guy is the guy who is going to marry them. Of course he's not. Young women shouldn't expect this to be the person they marry. They shouldn't have any fantasies or misconceptions. They shouldn't idealize who this person is who they're about to have a physical relationship with. And a woman shouldn't expect his experience to be anything similar to hers.

Adam: Normally, the earlier women lose it, the more they regret it, for the most part. It's something that is just a little more sacred to women than it is to guys. They usually end up either reliving it or regretting it or beating themselves up about it or having a little hostility about it.

You never get this one back, that first time out. For women, it's very important from a symbolic standpoint. Sure, you *could* lose your virginity at fourteen or fifteen and *maybe* be all right—but why not wait until eighteen? It couldn't hurt.

Dr. Drew: Guys need to develop the relationship before the physical intimacy. Girls need to choose guys who are capable of intimacy.

> **MYTHBUSTERS**
>
> **Myth:** *I'm still a virgin if he didn't orgasm inside me.*
>
> **The truth, according to Dr. Drew:** Virginity really involves penetration of the vagina by the penis. Beyond that, our culture today seems not to include other forms of sexuality within the definition of virginity, such as oral sex, and to some people, anal sex. I think there is a great deal of confusion about virginity and what it means. In the past, it typically referred to chastity. It seems that virginity has become a very individualized concept. Women want to retain some aspect of their sexuality as "special"; protecting this helps them feel worthwhile.

Q: Are guys immune to the kind of emotional upheaval women seem to have when they start having sex?

Dr. Drew: Not at all. With some guys, once they get into intimacy and it's their first time, they get connected—and they can get clingy if they're not fully developed and autonomous as people. Let me use myself as an example. I think I was sexually active too young and I became clingy, clingy, clingy.

ADAM's Theory: The Universal Hymen Plane

We've taken virginity and turned it into this sort of hybrid classification, a technical classification: I can technically be a virgin as long as a penis does not break the plane of my vagina.

Guys will remember Walter Payton, a great football player: When he would run with the ball, he'd be heading for the goal line, trying to lean that thing in just to break the plane of the goal line. A guy's penis is like Payton going for pay dirt, just trying to break the plane of the vagina.

But a woman will tell you that, as long as this plane is unbroken, as long as the penis does not cross the plane of the vagina, "I'm technically still a virgin and, as a virgin, I have these rights."

(I don't mean discounts to movies or anything, although this is something we should look into. Forget about students and seniors. If we really want to change society, we should start giving discounts to virgins: a couple of dollars off the bus, a few bucks off at the movies, maybe a free bucket of popcorn once you get into the theater. Imagine if we started affording opportunities to people who hung on to their virginity. We could give you your driver's license a year early. If you're a virgin, the legal drinking age is nineteen, not twenty-one. If you put these incentives in place and there was a way to check on it somehow, society would take a turn for the better.)

Technically a virgin—never mind that they've been having anal sex or giving hand jobs or blow jobs. Because the plane of the vagina has not been broken. That technicality lets them feel good about themselves, because they've held on to this chastity that they value.

So here's the deal: There should be not only the hymen, but the be-hymen (for anal sex) and the mouth hymen as well. There should be a sort of symbolic membrane in every orifice—even that circle you make when you touch your thumb to your index finger.

And when that membrane—physical or symbolic—is broken, then the deal is off. Then you're not a virgin.

Adam: How old were you?

Dr. Drew: I was sixteen, with someone my own age—and I wound up in an almost-six-year relationship with this person.

Adam: Because . . .

Dr. Drew: Because I got so connected. So enmeshed.

Adam: I'd probably still be with my first if she'd let me.

Dr. Drew: My first relationship was with somebody who I should have never been with in the first place. But you're a teenager and you don't know who you are and she doesn't know who she is. You get so intensely connected because of the sexual connection. And you can't handle it. You're there and you can't undo it. So you cling and cling and cling.

Q: I'm dying to have sex but am still a virgin at sixteen. I have a girlfriend who says she's not ready. All my friends are having sex and I feel like a failure. What should I do?

Adam: Really, my message to all virgins—in sex or in anything else—is this: Whatever it is, whether it's sex, flying a jet plane, bungee jumping: You already know what it feels like.

Dr. Drew: Right. You don't have to experience it to know what it feels like.

Adam: Think about what it feels like. That's what it feels like. I remember always wondering what a breast must feel like. What did it *feel* like? After I touched my first one, I thought, *Yeah, that's what I expected.*

What I'm saying is: It's nothing magical. People have turned sex into this mystical thing. When you tell a virgin about intercourse, oh, there's a whole aura around that. It takes it much further than just sort of imagining what a finger would feel like in your ear or in your ass. What I'm trying to say is, it's the same.

Yet a lot of guys think there's an extra something there. "Well, you know, jacking off is one thing, but *this* is . . ." Hey, you know what? Hump a Noxzema jar and close your eyes—and you ain't too far from it. You may be missing the emotional fun of it. But from a purely physical standpoint, the sensation is not as euphoric as your buddies who aren't virgins are making it out to be.

HOW TO HELP A FRIEND... *who is a virgin and worried about having sex*

Dr. Drew: If she's in the slightest bit of doubt, if virginity is something that she values, she needs to recognize that she's got to be clear that it's something that she's ready to give up. Is she a fourteen-year-old thinking of losing her virginity to a nineteen-year-old? Is the guy really a jerk?

Adam: You weigh the pros and the cons. But you certainly make sure it's her decision and that her nerves aren't due to the fact that he's the one pressuring her.

Dr. Drew: If you're seventeen and your friend has been in a relationship with a boyfriend for two years and they're thinking about having sex, I think you pat them on the back. You support them and talk to them about getting contraception. But if she's fourteen and he's twenty-seven, it's a whole different story. If it's a really bad situation, you tell the parents. Sometimes you have to sacrifice the friendship on behalf of saving the person.

Adam: You really use the same criteria whether it's her first guy or her twentieth guy. Is he committed? Is he a good guy? Does he have a criminal history?

Dr. Drew: Do you have contraception? Are you being honest with yourself about the fact that you're going to be sexually active?

Adam: Several billion people have gone through it before you. Even Mary eventually got nailed, didn't she, the Virgin Mary?

Dr. Drew: Supposedly not. That's why they call her the Virgin Mary. She was visited by a shaft of light one night—and it wasn't Joseph's.

Q: How do I know when it's time to become sexually active?

Dr. Drew: If it's not enjoyable to you and not an expression of your feelings about the other person and you're not reasonably comfortable, it's not the right time. The problem people have is denial about whether they're comfortable or not.

Adam: They don't know if they're going to enjoy it or not.

Dr. Drew: It should be something you look forward to, that you could move forward into as a natural part of the evolution of the feelings that two people have. It's not something you should get into with great ambivalence. And definitely not something you should do if it is to ensnare a man or to keep him happy.

Adam: People look at ambivalence as if they were speeding down the highway and coming to a fork. "Geez, I've got to turn right or left—but I can't stop."

But you can stop. If you have ambivalence—"Gee, I don't know if I'm going to like sex or not"—you probably are not ready to go.

If you have ambivalence about a homosexual relationship—"Gee, I don't know if I want to blow this guy"—you probably don't. And here's why:

If you really wanted to do it, if you're ready to go sexually with someone, you're *ready to go.* You're not going, *Oh, I don't know, maybe it's because he's not so attractive or because I haven't known him that long,* blah, blah, blah. When you're ready to go, gay or straight, you're *ready.*

Dr. Drew: Ambivalence is usually quite a substantial feeling. If it's not the right thing, it's not. Don't do it if it's not the right thing—but hang on, because it might become the right thing.

Q: Is it inevitable that the first time you have sex, it will be disappointing?

Adam: The analogy I make is to two people who see that Gap commercial, where the kids are swing-dancing. It looks great—so swinging, so cool. So they figure, "Hey, we can do this."

So they go out on the floor with the music playing, and they try one of those deals where the guy picks up the girl and throws her around except the guy pulls

DR. DREW

on Female Virginity and Becoming Sexually Active at a Young Age

Most women approach virginity as something to get over with. When they decide to have sex for the first time, they almost never enjoy the actual act. Expecting orgasmic function the first time is asking for disappointment.

The physical act of breaking the hymen while having intercourse for the first time can be comfortable with no bleeding—or it can be terribly uncomfortable, to the point of not being doable. There are even women who have to have the hymen surgically opened. In general, however, it is moderately uncomfortable, with a minimal amount of bleeding.

The earlier women initiate sexual activity, the less ready they are for the intense emotional experience it brings. Before the age of sixteen or seventeen, the emotional and neurobiological system simply are not

a groin muscle doing it. And the girl smashes her head on a lighting fixture. And it's not that dancing sucks but that you both need practice. You can't expect to win a dance contest your first time out.

But as you get into it, then it can be really exhilarating. You might even burn a few calories.

Q: Why does it seem to take women longer to learn to appreciate sex than men?

Adam: We're all born to what I call the "yummy" phase. We want only yummy. We don't want beer. We don't want caviar or whiskey or cigars. We don't want oral sex—or at least to be on the losing end of it. We want only things that taste good.

And then somewhere in our development, we make the transition to the acquired-taste stuff, whether it's vermouth martinis or whatever. But in general, women stay in the yummy phase longer than men. And that's why women aren't traditionally the big brandy drinkers, the big cigar smokers. They're into piña coladas, margaritas.

Dr. Drew: How does that correlate with sexuality?

Adam: I don't know what the correlation is. No, wait, here's the deal: I don't know that guys enjoy their first time around that much, because it's kind of like chugging the first six-pack. You don't even like the taste. But, later in life, you really enjoy beer. You learn to appreciate it. And I think women are the same way about guys. I don't think their first few times around, they can really appreciate it.

Q: Are kids starting to have sex at a younger age?

Dr. Drew: It's been about the same for the last ten years, I'd say.

Adam: It's leveled off. There's more experimentation, more threesomes, more wildness.

Dr. Drew: More same-sex experimentation. More bisexual stuff. And oral sex seems to have become a part of petting. For high-school-age kids now, the decision to make out with somebody is the decision to give a blow job for a girl. That's bizarre, I think. Adam goes on and on about how, when we were in high school, that was something that happened only to movie stars. It was almost deviant behavior. But we hear a lot about that, and it's taken very casually.

In a way, it's acknowledging that intercourse has more commitment attached to it. There's an emotional reaction to intercourse and there's a biology that you could regret, so they disarm the whole situation by doing this instead.

sufficiently developed. The act of sex creates a very intense bond between two people—but if you're fourteen and bond with an abusive seventeen-year-old, the results can be depressing and traumatic. Before the age of sixteen, most girls assume that the person they've decided to have sex with will be the person they are going to marry—an assumption that can lead to great pain and disillusionment because it's so seldom the case.

Think about how we refer to this: "I lost it to him," or "He took it from me." This should not be something lost or taken; it should be something shared out of the natural progression of an intimate relationship.

The most common problems we hear about related to the early loss of virginity include depression and loss of self-worth. Continued sexual promiscuity is one way they try to validate what they've done and act that out. Usually, abuse of some kind was perpetrated and these women continue to act on that.

Celebrity Input

★ from Actor Jon Cryer

Q: Aren't you guys afraid that by spreading all this information about sex you're just encouraging young people to be sexually active? Isn't that the wrong message?

> The earlier you begin having sex, the higher the risk of cervical cancer. The more partners you have, the higher the risk of cervical cancer. Warts and herpes, obviously, increase the risk of cervical cancer.

★ **Jon:** Young people are going to be sexually active. Young people are sexual beings. They should have the information to choose to or not. I personally think it's a bad idea to do it before you are psychologically ready. It's a lot bigger deal than people make of it.

Dr. Drew: I think our show is a sheep in wolves' clothes We're spreading the message about why young people shouldn't be sexually active, about why our culture should change. It's a way of getting people to learn that their actions have consequences, and to learn about those consequences, without preaching to them. How else are you going to hear that message except by listening to us? You've got to go into the trenches to talk to the people that are doing this in order to get their ears. They are already doing it. Those are the ones we're trying to talk to.

★ **Jon:** The litany of horror you hear every night is a testament to that.

Dr. Drew: Litany of horror. I like that.

Adam: I don't think it's ever wrong when people are intelligent enough to process that information. Listen, here it is. If you're intelligent, information is not going to hurt you—just like Marilyn Manson's not going to cause you to kill a family member. That's like saying that clean needles make people into junkies or that availability of condom machines makes teenage boys into rapists. Just because it's out there doesn't mean it's hurting or transforming society. We're here because they started it. Society . . . I mean. And if you are stupid, you really need information.

Dr. Drew: We're trying to turn the battleship around a little bit.

Adam: Otherwise the show would have been over and done with in the first three years.

Dr. Drew: Right. It wouldn't be pertinent.

ADAM's Rules for Who Is Not Allowed to Have Sex

Every time anyone has intercourse, they have the potential of bringing another life into the world. Most of the time, however, the people who fall into this category are too stupid to even contemplate parenthood. So, while you're all free to grope, grab, grind, and suck away, I don't want the following people running the risk of getting pregnant or getting someone else pregnant:

If you think you may be impregnated by having anal sex . . . **you're banned from having sex.**

If you haven't been the same since the New Kids on the Block broke up . . . **you're banned from having sex.**

If you think you may become impregnated by going into a Jacuzzi after your older brother had himself in there last summer . . . **you're banned from having sex.**

If you refer to your scrotum as your "nutsack" . . . **you're banned from having sex.**

If you think Depo-Provera is Geraldo's kid sister . . . **you're banned from having sex.**

If you pronounce vagina "vergina" . . . **you're banned from having sex.**

If you think that gravity is a contraceptive—in other words, if you believe your girlfriend can't get pregnant as long as she's on top . . . **you're banned from having sex.**

If people would stick to these rules, this world would be utopia.

5

Safe Sex

Young Drew: *I'm seventeen and I hear you guys talk all the time about condoms. How effective are those really as birth control? Are they okay?*

Adam: *Yeah, they're like, what is it, 80 to 90 percent?*

Dr. Drew: *Most of the failure is due to not being used properly. They don't roll it down, don't leave a reservoir at the tip. Have you used condoms yet?*

Young Drew: *Yeah, I use condoms but I don't think I'm using them right. I roll it down. They slip off sometimes.*

Dr. Drew: *You've got to hold them on the base when you pull out. You're seventeen now? How old is your girlfriend?*

Young Drew: *She's sixteen.*

Dr. Drew: *Is she able to be on the birth-control pill?*

Young Drew: *Oh, no, no way. She'd have to see a doctor and I'm afraid that her parents would find out.*

Dr. Drew: *Is this girl really into you? Are you in a close relationship?*

Young Drew: *Oh, yeah, we are totally in love. I'm absolutely committed to her.*

Adam: *Do you want to marry her?*

Young Drew: *No, of course not.*

Adam: *You don't? Why not?*

Young Drew: *Oh, that's so far-off. I can't even think about marriage. I'm too young.*

Adam: *Why don't you want to marry her?*

Young Drew: *I don't know if I ever want to get married. So, here's my question. I have to buy condoms and I'm always afraid somebody is going to see me when I buy them.*

Adam: *How have you been getting them so far?*

Young Drew: *I go to this pharmacy. I have to take a whole day; it takes me a while to get my nerve up. It's in Chinatown.*

Adam: *Wow. So you actually go to another part of town. That's kind of a brilliant idea. Not only is it a different area but all white people look the same to the Chinese, and there's just no way anyone you know will see you in Chinatown.*

Young Drew: *Let me ask you this. If you ejaculate into a condom once, can you keep going? Is that an okay way to use the condom?*

Dr. Drew: *No, absolutely not. It will slip off. You have to wash yourself. And wash your hands—wash everything.*

Adam: *You have to make a trip to Chinatown between each ejaculation. It sounds like you're so paranoid that even if she got a diaphragm you'd probably wear a condom anyway.*

Q: How do you define safe sex?

Dr. Drew: Safe sex, by definition, is abstinence. Everything else is risk reduction.

Adam: Yeah, but that's not sex, goofball. "Safe sex is abstinence." Drew, you've really got to think these things out. That's like saying, "What's the safest way to fly? Stay at home." Okay, thanks for the tip—but I've got to be in Portland tomorrow.

Dr. Drew: Beyond that, it's trying to put latex barriers between you and bodily fluids—your partner's fluids. That's really what it is.

Adam: Well, I'll be a little more lax and say that, sexually, there's always going to be some risk. There's risk in almost every endeavor in life, especially those that bring you pleasure. It's no coincidence that the greater the pleasure, the greater the rush, the greater the enthusiasm, the more danger. Bungee jumping is a bigger thrill than gardening because it's more dangerous. You can go to a go-cart track and putter around at ten miles an hour; it's okay and you're in no danger. But you get in a race car and go two hundred miles an hour: There's danger in that, but it's a much greater rush and a greater thrill.

Your job is to balance that. You might meet some transvestite crack addict at a rave some night and have unprotected, violent sex in the men's room and that could be an incredible thrill—but it's very dangerous. On the other hand, you could get checked out by the doctor and you could get the latex and the nonoxynol-9—not quite as thrilling, but very safe.

I think what you've got to do is figure out where your comfort zone is. You have to choose partners that don't have a real dangerous history and then you have to use protection appropriate to wherever you are in the relationship.

To me, safe sex could vary quite a bit. For instance, you should always use a condom—but if the person is a virgin and eighteen and has never been out of the house and you're the same and she's on the pill—well, I don't know how many virgins are on the pill—but the point is, you don't need the condom then, do you?

Dr. Drew: The school of thought is you can't trust anyone to tell you their true history.

Adam: But that's when people preach at other people to do what they want them to do. I've met a lot of women and you can size them up usually. You don't

ADAM's

Safe-Sex Inventions

The Condom Garter Belt: This is an elastic belt the man wears around his waist. It comes equipped with two alligator clips in the front, which are clamped on to the condom that's been rolled down to the base of the penis. It ends the worry of the condom accidentally slipping off during sex.

The Orthopedic Condom Garter Belt: This is the same idea, but with a lumbar support, about a four-to-six-inch strip along the lower back, for the extra support you need when you get a little older. You see guys at the warehouse stores, the home-supply stores, wearing these when they're doing heavy lifting. Same theory.

I've also modified it so that it can be impregnated with anticrab ointment. You snap it once on your right hip and that activates it.

The Condom Mud Flap: Get a little too much action going once you've got the condom in place?

want to have sex with them at a bar, but if you go out and you talk to a woman, you have a few drinks, you go out to dinner—you get a pretty good feel within the first couple of hours what her situation is, what her past is. You don't see any track marks on her arm—that kind of thing.

Q: What's the difference between safe sex and contraception?

Dr. Drew: They're not necessarily related. Even the condom that you use as a safe-sex tool isn't always a great contraceptive. It's supposed to be used with other barriers, like a sponge or diaphragm or something else.

Adam: But condoms are pretty good contraceptives.

Dr. Drew: Not bad. Not as good as the pill.

Q: What about types of sex where you don't use a condom?

Dr. Drew: Oral sex is always the question—and kissing. And they're potential risks. Very rare for transmission, but it's been documented.

Adam: Transmission of what?

Dr. Drew: HIV. Virtually any STD that is typically transmitted by genital-to-genital contact can be transmitted by oral-genital contact.

Q: Otherwise, is a condom the way to go in terms of disease prevention?

Dr. Drew: The latex condom is the single best means of obtaining protection against sexually transmitted disease. Animal-skin condoms tend to be permeable to viruses, though they're effective as a contraceptive.

Q: I have herpes. My girlfriend and I want to have sex, so I will wear a condom. Will this be safe?

Dr. Drew: It's never totally safe when there is an infectious disease involved. Herpes is terribly infectious when there is a virus being produced by the individual with the infection. Any symptom is a suggestion that the virus is being produced; the person then becomes highly contagious and even a condom probably wouldn't protect you.

The problem is you can't really tell when the virus is being produced. The condom is a reasonable barrier against transmission, though not totally effective. Obviously, fluid potentially containing a virus is touching other areas of the skin that aren't protected. So a condom affords some degree of protection, but it's not 100 percent.

Q: What do you do if you are married and one of the partners has herpes?

Dr. Drew: I've never encountered this in a clinical setting. I suspect that in married couples

Too much swinging and slapping going on? This condom mud flap would hang down from the bottom of the condom, to guard against backsplash or whiplash or what have you.

ADAM and DR. DREW on How to Put On a Condom

Adam: Basically, it's a clumsy, awkward process. It's akin to assembling a jungle gym on Christmas morning and you're missing a few nuts and bolts. That's especially true if the light's down low. Also, a lot of guys are scared they're going to lose a little something down there—and that they're not going to come back as strong.

But my feeling is that the process is quick and easy. And I really think guys should practice.

Dr. Drew: There's a school of thought that it should be rolled down a bit, so there's a reservoir on the tip. And you can put a little lubricant on the inside.

Adam: Just at the head though.

Dr. Drew: That will help with some of the feeling. It's supposed to increase some of the sensitivity.

Adam: The idea is that, when you put the lubricant on the end of your penis, you get the condom actually moving inside or on top. Get the action going.

Dr. Drew: Then the condom needs to be rolled all the way down to the base of the penis. And when you pull out, you need to hold the base of the condom so it doesn't slip off the penis.

where one of the individuals has herpes, they do what they can, but that ultimately they both probably just end up getting it. For the man it really has no significance whatsoever, except it's a nuisance, unless there are very, very frequent outbreaks. For women, it increases the risk of cervical cancer. It complicates delivery of a baby somewhat.

There are very effective medications to suppress viral production, such as Famvir, Valtrex, and Zovirax. If somebody is terribly concerned about infecting their partner, the risk can be further reduced by taking medication that decreases the potential of outbreak and/or viral production.

Q: Is there any way I can have sex and get away with not using a condom?

Dr. Drew: It's lunacy in this day and age, to my way of thinking. People focus on AIDS, but there are a multiplicity of sexually transmitted diseases out there, which are more common and could be equally as disturbing and quite dangerous. So why would a guy not wear a condom?

Adam: To a guy, sexually, there's a window of opportunity, at least initially. It's like a business transaction that's going on—when you get a really good deal on some vagina. You're making out like a bandit and the phone rings or—

Dr. Drew: And you don't want her to think twice about it.

Adam: Any distractions—such as stopping to put on a condom—and you might not be able to close the deal. That's why a lot of guys don't do it. When they're about to have sex, guys are almost hysterical, in the sense that it's like somebody who's fleeing a burning building—and you're trying to tell them to remember a coat because it's cold outside.

Q: Do condoms decrease sexual sensitivity?

Adam: That's not true. I don't think the comfort thing is as big an issue as guys make it out to be.

Dr. Drew: There are some guys who lose an erection when they put on a condom. They can't function sexually for whatever reason. But I don't think any woman should accept that as a reason why the guy shouldn't wear one. It should be a deal-breaker: If he won't wear one, the deal's off.

One technique to overcome this is putting a water-based lubricant on the tip of the penis before you put on the condom.

MYTHBUSTERS

Myth: *All condoms are equally effective in protecting against STDs and AIDS.*

The truth, according to Dr. Drew: Animal-skin condoms are clearly not as effective against the viral STDs. They have microscopic pores that allow the virus to penetrate. The polyurethane or latex condoms appear to be the only safe barriers available presently. Still, they are not 100 percent effective because they have their own failure rate and must be used properly.

Q: My girlfriend thinks condoms take the romance out of sex. What should I do?

Dr. Drew: Some people are uncomfortable with having to plan for sex. Then it's more of an acknowledged reality. Women, particularly, do this. If they have to plan, if they have to go out and get birth-control pills or condoms, then they really have to acknowledge to themselves that they're sexually active. When, in their mind, in their heart, they want to be a virgin. Yet they're not and they have difficulty reconciling that with themselves. It implies things about them and their worth. So they don't even want to admit it to themselves.

Adam: It's like premeditated sex is the same as "First-Degree Whore."

Dr. Drew: But hey, you know what? If you're feeling that way, then don't do it. If you're not prepared to admit it to yourself, don't do it.

MYTHBUSTERS

Myth: *Two condoms are better than one.*

The truth, according to Dr. Drew: This couldn't be further from the truth. In fact, two condoms are more likely to cause friction against one another and actually break. That is much more likely than with a single condom, properly used.

Also, young people have a kind of magical way of thinking. They believe that they can't die; they believe nothing can happen to them. "I wasn't really having sex. This guy just put his penis in me but we weren't really having sex."

Adam: It's the same thing I used to do when I had a term paper due Monday morning and it was still Friday afternoon. I was out of there, man. I mean, Monday may never come around. A tidal wave could hit Sunday night. There could be a Russian invasion. But damned if that Monday didn't always roll around.

Q: Why wouldn't a woman require a guy to wear one?

Dr. Drew: They think, *Oh, the guy won't like me if I ask him to.* Or, *He'll think that I think there's something wrong with him.* Or, *If I do it to protect him, he'll think there's something wrong with me.*

Adam: Guys do the same thing. They're maybe embarrassed to bring up the condom thing. Like the women will take offense with that, when actually it's just common courtesy.

Dr. Drew: Yet people will also say, "Oh, I forgot to use a condom."

Adam: I don't believe anyone ever forgets anything, much less a condom. And here's why you shouldn't take that risk.

It's like you're in Vegas at the craps table and you're on the hottest roll of your life. But somebody wants you to go back up to your room because the toilet is dripping and you need to shake the handle a couple of times. Now there's a real good chance that the thing will stop dripping on its own. But there's a chance—a very small chance—that the thing's going to flood and destroy not only your luggage but the room downstairs, and that you're going to be held responsible. Still, it's just a small chance—say, 5 percent.

Dr. Drew: But it's too big a price.

Adam: I'll tell you what most guys would do. They'd let it ride, man. Hey, you're on a roll!

Q: How do you change that?

Adam: In a situation like that, the woman has to be the pit boss. They have to hold the dice. Sorry—no dice. No dice today. No dice.

Dr. Drew: Men, when they're on a roll sexually, have a momentum biologically that is overwhelming. And women don't, necessarily. Their brain is still functioning. Men's brains don't function very well at that point. The only reason a woman would have not to bring it up—not to say, "Wait, let's use a condom"—is that she's afraid she's going to be rejected by the guy. Well, let him. Let him get pissed off. If the guy gets pissed off, screw him. He doesn't care about her anyway.

Adam: The day guys wear condoms willingly is the day there's something in it for them. That's the day when women tell them that if they don't, they aren't getting any.

Dr. Drew: That's what it boils down to. If women require it. And the only way women are going to require it is if they A) assert themselves, and B) acknowledge to themselves what they're doing.

Q: Who is supposed to bring the condom?

Dr. Drew: Everybody.

Adam: I agree. It's important for everyone to have one. Unfortunately, when a woman pulls a condom out of her purse, guys think, *Okay, here's someone who's done this before.*

Dr. Drew: That's horrible.

Adam: I know, but it's true. Would you agree? I think women should always have one. And they probably should wait for the guy to make the move for his. If it doesn't look like he's going to—

Dr. Drew: —then they should be outraged.

Adam: No, here's what they should do. They should say it came with the purse. In fact, that would be great: Every wallet and every purse sold in America should just come with a condom in it. If every handbag and every wallet came with a condom, then the condom would just be in the purse. It wouldn't be as if the woman reached into her nightstand and grabbed a handful before she headed out on the date. Same with the guy. "Oh, look what I brought on the date."

See, the problem with the condom is that people do not get a verbal agreement ahead of time about sex. They don't say, "Would you like to proceed with intercourse?"

"Affirmative."

"Okay, sign here."

So the person who makes the first move for the condom sometimes is being a little presumptuous.

Dr. Drew: As though they planned to have sex ahead of time, even if they didn't know whether they would or not. And what does that mean?

Adam: But that wouldn't be a problem if every purse and every wallet came with condoms sewn right into them.

Q: How do you ask someone for their sexual history?

Adam: I'm not a huge fan of this. I think you go out on a date with a person and you get to know them as a person. You ask them questions, like were they popular in high school. Where did they go to college? Did they this, did they that? What did they do after college?

Dr. Drew: What about junior college?

Adam: Junior college—all bets are off.

But really, you start talking to her: You ask her about high school and she'll say, "I was on the cheerleading squad," and you'll say, "Betcha drove the boys crazy," and she'll say something like, "Nope, never had a date in high school," or "Well, I had a boyfriend from ninth grade all through high school until I moved away to college." You can generally get a pretty good feel from that.

Dr. Drew: Can you really believe those histories, though? Especially early on in a relationship, when she's trying to impress you? I mean, think of all the stuff we have to crack through just to get to the truth. The average guy or girl doesn't know how to do that.

Q: What questions should you be asking?

Dr. Drew: A better question would be: How about your dad?

Adam: Yeah, that's a good way to go.

Dr. Drew: How do you feel about Dad? Where's he been? How did that affect you? How do you like Mom? Do you spend time with your parents?

Adam: "Where's your dad?"

"He's dead."

"Are you upset?"

"Yeah, because he didn't die soon enough."

"Okay, waiter—a couple of condoms here."

Q: I'm about to get intimate with someone new. What do I say if she asks for a sexual history and I've slept around a lot?

Adam: Do you want sex or not? Ask yourself that—and if the answer is yes, then you lie.

Look, if I'm a guy who's slept around and I've had unprotected sex and I've never had the dignity for me or my partners to get tested—what a scumbag! Basically, the whole reason I've slept with so many women is because I've learned to lie my little ass off. There's no way you're getting a straight answer from this guy.

A better approach is to note that he's wearing a monogrammed ascot and he's smoking a Tiparillo and he smells of Aqua Velva and he drives a Pontiac Fiero that has a kit on it so it looks like a Testarosa. These are all better indications that you should be using a condom than asking Serge there what his sexual history is. I mean, it couldn't hurt to ask. But it's catch-22: The guy has slept around a lot and hasn't used protection and hasn't gotten tested. So this is a guy who's going to look you in the eye and lie.

Dr. Drew: That's the fundamental part: Know the person. You wouldn't buy a car without investigating it first. Yet a person you're about to have sex with, you take on impulse? It's the most untrustworthy impulse in the world.

Adam: You've got to trust your instincts, not what the information the person is giving you in a sexual history. It's like if someone shows up at your door and says, "My minivan broke down. I have a group of Christian kids who are late for camp and I'd like to come in and use the phone." Now if it's a guy with, I don't know, a priest's collar, you would let him into your house. But if it's an eight-foot biker with shackles hanging from his ankles and an orange jumpsuit, forget about the information he's giving you about the van and the kids: He's a guy you shouldn't let into your house. And it's not because of what he's telling you—it's the fact that he's disheveled and he's got a cold sweat going and he smells of Pabst Blue Ribbon. You just know you're in for a good raping and beating if you let him in.

Q: What about when it's not that obvious?

Adam: The reason these guys are probably racking up the numbers is because they're good at lying. In that case, you just refer back to the condom and let discretion be the better part of valor.

Dr. Drew: You notice we're really talking mostly about how women deal with men. Women just need to trust their instincts and demand that the relationship get built first before they have sex. Then they'll know whether or not they want to sleep with the guy, whether it's appropriate.

Adam: But the same thing applies to men dealing with women. If they've got that "come-and-get-it" tattoo on their ass or the black fingernail polish and fifteen piercings in one nostril, well, you just know. Just ask them what bands they're into. If they say, "I subscribe to the Mostly Mozart Festival," they're in—put them down for oral sex. If they want to see Marilyn Manson, get out the condom. If you go out and meet a woman at a bar and ask her to dance and, ten minutes into it, her hand is rubbing your groin out on the dance floor, go ahead and assume she's been with a couple of partners.

Dr. Drew: Yes, but in that situation, most guys are going to go, "Oh God, this is great!"

Adam: So you use the condom.

Dr. Drew: But maybe you shouldn't be having sex with somebody like that at all.

Adam: Drew, I know you're on your own personal crusade. But if you go out with a woman and you're having sex the night you meet her, then there's a better chance than not that you should use a condom. Like I said, you should always use a condom, but you should be able to assess high and low risk.

If you just meet a chick at a bar and she says, "Let's do some heroin and then have sex," use the condom.

If you meet a woman and it takes you 17 dates and $35,000 before you even get a kiss, then that's an argument for a much lower-risk situation.

DR. DREW on Why History Taught Us to Be Wary of Sex

For thousands of years, if you had multiple sex partners, you died. You got sexually transmitted diseases and you died: pelvic inflammatory disease, gonorrhea, syphilis—they could all kill you.

So if you are a parent of a teenager and you love your child, what are you going to do? You've been a teenager yourself. You know the intense biology operating there. How do you keep your child from killing him- or herself with sex?

What you do is create a society with rules to contain them, so they don't die. That's why society has sexual mores—because otherwise your child would go out and not only have sex but put his or her life in danger.

If you had a boy, he could contract an STD—syphilis, gonorrhea. And he would die.

And if you had a girl, she could get also pregnant. That in itself was bad enough because society condemned it. Plus you had a child on your hands, another mouth to feed without any economic benefit. Worse, if she got pregnant, she could die. A significant percentage of women died at childbirth until only a hundred years ago. Which is where the notion of women as the weaker sex came from.

Which is why specific religions and society as a whole came up with these rules of sexual behavior that said, essentially, No! Don't have sex! Sex is bad. Sex is evil. If you break these rules, you will be severely punished.

Because it was a way of deterring young people from what was, for a long time, inherently dangerous behavior.

6

Teen Pregnancy

Celebrity Input

★ *from Actress Janeane Garofalo*

★ ★ ★ **Q: I'm a thirteen-year-old girl and I just found out that I'm pregnant. Do I tell my parents in order to get an abortion? They'll freak out. What do I do?**

★ **Janeane:** Well, one would hope that you are in a position to discuss these things with your parents. Hopefully, antiquated statements like "My dad will throw me out of the house" and stuff like that are a thing of the past. Because I hate to even think about parents withholding their love at a time when their kids need them the most.

Dr. Drew: Unfortunately, though, people do sometimes. I'm not sure on the legalities in all of the states. I think most states require you to be fourteen to have

ADAM says: You Know You're Ready to Be a Parent If . . .

- Your braces will be off in time for the delivery.
- Your dad will let you borrow the car long enough to get to the delivery room.
- You own a No. 2 pencil to fill out lengthy welfare paperwork.
- You can find a sitter so you can go to the junior prom.
- You can call off the search for your birth dad long enough to find the guy who knocked you up.

medical care without consent of the parent. So a thirteen-year-old is right at the cusp here.

Adam: I think for girls it's a more traumatic thing than they may anticipate. I think there is a psychological aspect of this procedure that lingers on long after the medical end of this procedure has been performed. We hear about it all the time. There is an emotional side of it that they weren't ready to deal with. So if you don't tell your mom or dad, you should certainly get your friends to be with you and support you.

★ **Janeane:** I wish you didn't absolutely have to have consent because that's probably what keeps some teens waiting too long.

Dr. Drew: That's absolutely true, because their denial systems are so intense that they cause themselves to just go into hiding. It's like, "Well, I'll deal with it later," and suddenly it's seven months.

★ **Janeane:** And suddenly you are at the prom. And then look what happens—it's a big mess.

Dr. Drew: Unfortunately, here's the reality: If you are under seventeen and you have a pregnancy, you need the support of all the important people in your life. And yes, they may be angry; yes, they may be outraged. Believe me, more often than not, they're going to blame themselves. Which probably will piss you off even more. But you have to tell your parents. You have to at thirteen and you should at fourteen, fifteen, sixteen. Even the most abusive, obnoxious parents are going to rally behind a child in serious need like this.

Adam: I don't know about rally behind, but they may pull it together for a day to give you a ride to the clinic. You know abusive, bad parents, I don't hold out much hope for them.

Q: Can you be pregnant and not know it?

Dr. Drew: Maybe. That seems to be a common phenomenon among teenage women. It's more often acute denial than ignorance.

Adam: Even if they do think they're pregnant, for a lot of these kids there's no way they're talking to their folks. Because they think if they say to their folks, "Gee, how long do you have to wait before you get an over-the-counter pregnancy test?" a little bulb will go off above the parent's head. They're scared to talk to their doctor because they don't even really have one and even if they did, they think the doctor is basically a puppet for their folks. As for this whole BS about the counselor at school, I don't know if it's anything like when I was in school, but if I saw my counselor coming down the hall, I turned the other way. I wouldn't dream in a million years of talking to any of these uptight people about any personal problems.

How to Help a Friend... *who discovers she's pregnant at seventeen*

Dr. Drew: You take her to health care, first of all. Don't let her deny what has happened. Help her deal with it and confront it, as painful as that can be. And that includes going down to the family planning center and looking at her options. Most important of all, be available for the person to support her and not judge her. Don't make the decisions for her but just be available. Also, make sure she doesn't succumb to denial, so that she doesn't really confront the situation until the sixth month.

Adam: That's the main thing—that she do something. Teenagers love to deny stuff and they love to sit on stuff—to hope that it goes away. There are options—including abortion—but those options are things she needs to think about before she's too far along.

Dr. Drew: Also, encourage the involvement of a trusted adult, whether it's a sibling or a parent or whoever.

Q: Where can an underage person get contraception?

Dr. Drew: I don't know any age limit on purchasing condoms. And, in most states, fourteen is the age at which a youngster is able to have confidential health care without parental involvement. So if you wish to get oral contraceptives or whatever, you can get them in a confidential way from a physician, or from any of the family planning organizations that are around.

★ *from Writer-Director-Performer Keenen Ivory Wayans*

★ ★ ★ ★ **Q: My boyfriend and I were having anal sex and the condom came off. Can I get pregnant from anal sex?**

Dr. Drew: I think they are obviously worried about things dripping down somewhere and that kind of thing. Anybody who's ever become impregnated or is the product of such a pregnancy, please step forward. I've never met anybody like that. I don't think it's ever happened. I've never heard of such a thing in any way. Obviously the colon is a totally separate system from the uterus.

★ **Keenen:** The fact that she's not sure whether her ovaries are connected to her asshole is really frightening. I mean it's like . . .

Adam: She's got to listen to that "shin bone's connected to the leg bone" song a little more carefully the next time. I guess that makes the question: If she did get pregnant, where would the baby come out? The thing that's interesting about these questions, and this is part of the trouble this country is in, is you have people having sex and potentially having children who are this uninformed.

★ **Keenen:** I know. Her question should be presented to Congress because it really says how bad we need sex education in school.

Adam: If you ask that question, you should be a good five to eight years away from having sex—from the time in life you figure out the answer to that question. Even if it's at twenty-seven, you shouldn't be able to get it on until thirty-five.

MYTHBUSTERS

Myth: *If I didn't ejaculate inside her, she can't get pregnant.* Or: *Pulling out is an effective method of birth control.*

The truth, according to Dr. Drew: There are emissions prior to ejaculation that sometimes contain high concentrations of sperm. But you'll have no sensation of ejaculating when they come out. So so whether you ejaculate or not, any penetration without contraception could result in pregnancy.

Q: Do some young people get pregnant on purpose?

Dr. Drew: At least quasi-intentionally. They're not getting in the way of becoming pregnant. They're trying to inject some comfort back into their lives, some meaning. They want something to love, something that loves them—which is the absolute worst reason to have a child.

Adam: They want a pet.

Dr. Drew: Exactly. And those people end up with the most disturbed kinds of children because the needs of the child are never met. It's always the mother's needs that come first. The baby is not a person to them; it's an extension of them. It's there for their emotional needs—but it's a separate person who is going to be damaged by these teen mothers. If you're not developed as a human being, how can you be available emotionally for a baby? They don't understand that they're damaging another person. And that's not to mention their inability to provide for and effectively cope with the basic needs of the child.

Adam: Well, they always say, "Everything will be all right when I look into the eyes of my baby." Yeah, right.

MYTHBUSTERS

Myth: *I can't get pregnant if I'm having sex in a swimming pool or Jacuzzi.*

The truth, according to Dr. Drew: Believe me, pregnancy is just as possible in the water as it is on dry land. There is a myth that somehow the temperature of the Jacuzzi might decrease a man's effectiveness. While overheating the testicles might decrease a man's fertility over time, having sex in a Jacuzzi is a far cry from using a contraceptive.

Q: Suppose they are ready to have empathy for their child?

Dr. Drew: Yes, but a lot of kids we talk to, when we ask where they're going to live, they say, "With my parents." They miss the whole point that they're the parents now; they're not the child anymore.

Adam: It's absolutely pathetic how they look at that as some kind of independence. If we ask how they're going to raise the child, they say, "I'm going to go to college and work." Yeah, but how are you going to do that and take care of the kid? "Well, my mom will do it." It's more like a hobby than a commitment: "Yeah, well, I'm not going to let it throw off my schedule."

People need to be scared to have kids: scared financially and scared emotionally.

Dr. Drew: When somebody is there to take care of you, you never really learn to take care of yourself. If people didn't know there was someone there to support them if they had a baby, they would address the reality of how they were going to support the child. And they wouldn't have it in the first place.

Q: Which presents more physical problems for a young woman: an early pregnancy or an abortion?

Adam: Pregnancy.

Dr. Drew: By a slight margin. Pregnancy itself has a lot of risks. They're both pregnancy, really; one just terminates. The risks of major complications are higher with pregnancy. Although the risks of infertility obviously are higher with abortion. Certainly, the risks of taking oral contraceptives are substantially less than the risks of pregnancy.

Q: What about the abortion vs. adoption question?

Adam: Here's my bumper sticker: "Your aborted fetus could be the next president—but probably not." The problem is that the people who are mature enough to give up a kid for adoption aren't the ones getting pregnant and aren't the ones being horrid parents. It's almost a catch-22: If you have the decency to say, "I could not give this child the love and attention that a child needs"—it's almost that you're a good parent by virtue of the fact that you're giving it up for adoption.

And it's almost always the people who are in zero position to have a kid who say, "Adoption is out of the question." Meanwhile, we've got a lot of religious folks—oops, she got pregnant in a threesome and doesn't know which one is the father. An abortion? "Well, I don't think that's morally right." But what about the threesome? Where does that fall? I mean, you're picking and choosing your morality here: "Well, this part of the Bible works for me because my neighbor doesn't have an oxen. But this other part about his wife—I'm digging his wife."

MYTHBUSTERS

Myth: *You can't get pregnant during your period.*

The truth, according to Dr. Drew:
You can get pregnant at any time, any place. Any time there has been penetration, there can be pregnancy. It is impossible to predict when a viable egg is available in the fallopian tube for conception.

Q: I was having sex and my boyfriend's condom slid right off. What should I do?

Dr. Drew: That's a condom failure. That's where your condom garter belt comes in, Adam.

Adam: Right. It's a long piece of elastic with alligator clips on each end; it stretches around your waist and attaches to the condom on either side.

Dr. Drew: It's common for condoms to fail. Condoms get caught up inside of women, too, and people freak out about it. Not uncommonly, doctors are called upon to retrieve these things.

Q: My boyfriend and I were having sex and the condom tore. Does this mean I'm pregnant?

Dr. Drew: You could be. It's certainly very possible.

Adam: It's like saying, "Well I was wearing a crash helmet while I was riding the motorcycle but it blew off right before I got in an accident. Is anything going to happen to me?"

Dr. Drew: Yeah. Is my head more likely to get hurt?

Adam: It's as if you didn't have the goddam thing on. I had that condom on all the time—right up until I came.

Q: What should I do if, on the spur of the moment, my boyfriend and I have sex without a contraceptive?

Dr. Drew: Even if you do have unprotected sex, there is a morning-after pill—they're very effective, leaving only about a 30 percent chance of pregnancy. But they need to be used within 72 hours of sexual contact.

Q: Is there a psychological reason not to use a contraceptive?

Dr. Drew: Not a good one.

Adam: It's like you have a book from the library that is overdue and someone says, "Well, the library is across town and you can return it." But they might have screwed up the paperwork and not even know that you have it. So you mean I'm driving across town to return this thing and they may be surprised when I walk in?

Dr. Drew: In other words, well, I might *not* be pregnant.

Adam: I can tell you, when I was seventeen, I would have had all my money riding on "She's not pregnant." Unless those pills are sitting right on the nightstand, I think if you've got a seventeen-year-old and the condom breaks with his girlfriend, he's not going to say, "Oh, my God, let's call the doctor." I think it's pretty much that he'll sit around rubbing the rosary beads.

Dr. Drew: Everybody who has adolescent children ought to give them a packet of these morning-after pills to keep around, even if they're not taking the pill all the time. The research suggests that taking these morning-after pills—Lo/Ovral and Ovral and others—will suppress ovulation, rather than causing an abortion.

Adam: If I had a seventeen-year-old daughter and she had a boyfriend, I'd say, "Listen . . ."

Dr. Drew: You'd say, "Go on the pill." If she said no, you'd say, "Well, keep these, they might reduce the risk of pregnancy."

Unfortunately, denial is a big problem. That kind of magical thinking that "it's not going to happen to me."

Adam: Plus the idea that in nine months you might have a baby—geez, nine months is an eternity. It might as well be the first day of school and you're thinking about what you'll be doing next summer. Forget it; you can barely think ahead to Christmas vacation.

So here's all I'm saying: It has to be made as easy as possible for kids to get contraceptives. When we start saying, "Well, we're not going to have condoms in the schools," or here or there—or we're saying, "You need a note from your parents to get these," forget it.

So what do we do? We've got to stop the kids from having kids.

Q: What do you make of the recent epidemic among teenage women who hide their pregnancies, then secretly deliver babies and either abandon them or, worse, kill them? It's been particularly newsworthy in New Jersey, but seems to be happening everywhere.

Adam: First off, I'd like to say that, if I was governor of New Jersey, I would install incubators in all public facilities to discourage disgruntled teens when they try to do away with their preemies. Station nurses in them as well.

Dr. Drew: That's just symptomatic of how aggressive, violent, and depraved these people are—and how detached they are from the reality of these separate beings having separate existences and feelings.

Adam: To me, the problem almost solves itself. I know it seems like a great tragedy to many but, to me, when you have a mom who is sort of toying with the idea of throwing you in a Dumpster at birth, well, even if she doesn't, I'm not sure you're going to get that car seat or braces or the private school and college education. After all, this is someone who's toying with tossing you into a Dumpster.

Dr. Drew: When they actually raise the children, in some respects it's even worse because the child becomes a specific extension of them, someone who's just there to meet their narcissistic needs. If their narcissistic needs are such that they want the baby gone, it's: "Oh well, he's dead—I didn't want him anyway. I shouldn't have gotten pregnant."

What these girls are saying is: "This is me; it's all an extension of me. I can do what I want." If you really follow that logic, it's: "It was inside me a few seconds ago, but it's premature anyway and I could have had it taken out."

Society tells the young woman that the fetus is hers, part of her body. A small leap of logic leads her to conclude it is only slightly different when it's outside her uterus.

Adam: There are three mind-sets here and they're all dangerous: First, "This baby is a piece of me and I can do with it what I want." Second, "I'm not going to give it up for adoption because it's a piece of me." And third, "I've had this child—now who's going to give me the money to take care of him?" I blame Reebok more than I blame Gloria Steinem—that whole "It's your world" mentality.

Q: What effects will the teen pregnancy epidemic have on society as a whole?

Dr. Drew: This is the issue—this is it, the one that will affect the existence of society beyond the next hundred years. In the next twenty years alone, one third of the country could be screwed-up; they're going to be characterologically disturbed people.

Adam: It's crime, unemployment, pollution . . .

Dr. Drew: . . . drug abuse, violence . . .

Adam: . . . infrastructure, welfare, government. It's all coming apart—and it's all directly affected by this.

You know what this actually is? This is like El Niño—it really is. Everyone is harping about El Niño—and I'll tell you what El Niño is. The water temperature in the oceans goes up a degree and a half. Yeah? So who gives a shit? Well, *you* should, because when the ocean heats up, El Niño comes and all hell breaks loose.

The point is that something as benign as the ocean's temperature rising a couple of degrees turns into mass devastation with hurricanes and heat spells and blizzards and floods, whether it's for farmers in the Midwest or the fishermen on the coasts or Johnny Carson's house over in Malibu. The point is that it just keeps going and going and going—and the effects are felt.

Dr. Drew: All of these unwanted babies grow up to have more kids as teenagers. Their kids typically become either abusers or victims of abuse.

Adam: They then fill the prisons, then come out of prison and go on welfare because they're uneducated, so they can't compete in the job market, putting more and more of a burden on a smaller and smaller group of taxpayers.

A woman who has a kid in, say, the tenth grade, will usually have another kid before she has graduated from high school, by eighteen or so. Then she rolls from abusive guy to abusive guy. The next thing you know, she's thirty and she's got a couple of teenagers who've never worked a day in their lives. They don't have any education because they've basically been chained to the TV—and they go out and get some other teenage girl pregnant and start the whole thing all over again.

Dr. Drew: I've heard data that a shocking percentage of the babies born in America will be born to teenagers.

Adam: By definition, the number will go even higher in years to come, because the children of teenagers are more likely to get pregnant as teenagers.

Dr. Drew: They do what their parents do because they're not healthy emotionally. They don't have the right instinct toward nurturing and stability.

Adam: And, eventually, the wheels come off the wagon. So that's basically what we think about teen pregnancy.

I've been saying this from the beginning and Drew has been with me. I won't just say teen pregnancy—I'm saying anyone of any age—when they have unwanted kids who are improperly cared for, it will destroy society eventually. Look at any society that is coming apart and I'll show you a whole bunch of kids who need a whole lot of help without anyone around to take care of them. You can mark the health of a society by how many kids there are per caring adult.

DR. DREW on Methods of Contraception

The oral contraceptive ("the pill"): In most states a woman can get the oral contraceptive pill without parental consent from age fourteen. The pill basically tricks your body to believe that it's pregnant so you don't release an egg from the ovary. So the egg has no possibility of being fertilized. It is 99+ percent effective.

Among the side effects are midcycle bleeding or loss of your period. Your doctor can adjust the dose to reinstate a normal menstrual cycle. Other possible side effects include nausea and water retention. But the pill has not been proven to be associated with cancer.

The pill has no long-term effects on fertility. Once you stop taking the pill, you should be potentially fertile again within six months.

Norplant: This is essentially the same kind of birth control as the pill, except that it is implanted in your arm, with a time-release mechanism that lasts three to five years.

Depo-Provera: This is a shot women receive, which covers three months of birth control. It does tend to cause abnormal bleeding—sometimes up to the entire three months after the first shot. Usually this will subside following the second injection.

Barrier methods: These include condoms, contraceptive sponges, and diaphragms. Typically, for a barrier method to be as effective as hormonal therapy such as the pill, you need to use multiple barriers: a condom and a sponge, or a condom and a diaphragm.

Intrauterine devices, or IUDs: These are effective, though they can cause some physical problems, such as cramping. And they're not recommended for women who have never been pregnant, because they are thought to increase the risk for infection getting into the fallopian tubes and causing fertility problems. So they're not really workable for young women who are just becoming sexually active.

The rhythm method: Unworkable and undependable. Ovulation fluctuates even within a woman's own cycle, depending on things such as diet and stress. So the bottom line is that you can literally get pregnant at any time of the month.

Withdrawal: Completely ineffective. Prior to ejaculation, the male secretes what is known as preseminal fluid, the so-called *pre-cum,* which has a high concentration of sperm. And there's no telling in advance when that's going to ooze out.

7

Promiscuity

Q: How do you define promiscuity?

Adam: That's a good question.

Dr. Drew: I'm wondering what his definition is. I suppose mine would be having sex with different people.

Adam: The definition of promiscuity is set by society.

Q: It's not just sex with multiple partners?

Dr. Drew: It is that. But it's that and something else.

Adam: It's about 80 percent set by society and about 20 percent what kind of pace you normally would be on and what your pace is now. It's basically a societal thing: If society says, "Listen, if you're with ten people in a month, you're promiscuous," then, if you're with ten people in a month, well, you're promiscuous. At least according to society. You may not feel promiscuous—but who cares what you feel?

Dr. Drew: I suppose the definition has changed from the sixties through the seventies and eighties and now the nineties. There's been a change in the quality of people's perceptions over the years. When people were talking about being promiscuous in the eighties, they were talking about forty or fifty partners. Now you hear people say, "I'm promiscuous"—and they're talking about ten partners. Wouldn't you say ten is the number now that people seem to equate with promiscuity?

Adam: Well, no. It depends on how old you are.

Dr. Drew: Okay, for young people, young adults.

Adam: If you talk to a sixteen-year-old guy and he's dating a sixteen-year-old girl and she's been with four guys, he's devastated. If you want to know what a guy is going to consider promiscuous and be upset about, you can figure it out with this kind of math. Most guys will be upset if you exceed this equation:

[Your age – 15] × 2 = workable. But times 3 = trouble.

How to Help a Friend... *who is becoming too promiscuous*

Adam: It's not really about, "Hey, knock it off, Horny." It's more about whatever it is they're acting out.

Dr. Drew: Look for the reasons and try to get them to identify and maybe solve them. Ask them, "What's bothering you? What's going on? Why is this happening?" Be available to that person and try to give them a safe environment to express this. They may not be able to—most teenagers can't. They may be a million years away from their feelings about it, or in denial about it. Or they may be doing drugs. But understand that usually it's a symptom of something that's bothering them that they can't talk about, but instead are acting out.

Q: Is promiscuous behavior as simple as pleasure-seeking? Or is there something more destructive at work?

Dr. Drew: I think promiscuity has more to do with destructive, physical relationships and acting out. Destructive in the sense that it distresses somebody, doesn't make them feel good about themselves. It makes them feel bad. Or it's acting out: It's an impulsive thing that comes from some unresolved emotional conflict. So it has no direction to it. It's not gratifying, it's not purposeful—it's trying to avoid feelings more than anything else. It's like using a drug.

Adam: But a lot of people can go a little wild for a few years without it meaning there's something wrong with them. There's a phase that most people go through in their life—male and female, maybe between nineteen and twenty-four—where they really rack up the numbers. Abused, nonabused, it doesn't matter. It's just something that happens.

Most women, if you catch them before eighteen or nineteen, they haven't had a lot of activity. But squeeze five or six years in there—between nineteen and twenty-five, that's when it's most likely to happen.

Dr. Drew: That's probably biology working itself out.

Adam: So I don't think you can chalk it all up to acting out.

Dr. Drew: You're right. There are people you wouldn't consider that promiscuous because it's the norm. And normative behavior is set by the social climate.

Q: How often is promiscuity related to sexual abuse?

Dr. Drew: It routinely is related to that. When people are sexually abused, they become almost overly active, sort of what people identify as nymphomaniacal. That's a term that really has no application anymore; we just view them as sexual compulsives. They masturbate frequently, start at a young age, have a lot of partners. It's almost as if the brain evolves in a way it isn't supposed to and gets stuck there. Or they become averse to sex; they can't do it at all. They stay away from it because it's very ungratifying. But, actually, it's ungratifying either way.

Q: How many partners is too many?

Dr. Drew: That's changed with the coming of AIDS. Guys will be worried that their girlfriend is promiscuous because she's slept with maybe ten guys. Adam's reaction is that ten partners isn't really that many. In Adam's head, he's thinking forty or fifty. Because that's the way it was in the eighties.

Fear of AIDS lowers the number. I really believe that. It's always about that: What does it mean about the person and their risk to me, in terms of biology?

Adam: It's like anything. There's a general awareness campaign about AIDS that's been launched on society, that wasn't around for the twenty years between 1967 and 1987.

Celebrity Input

★ *from Greg Camp of Smashmouth*

Q: While my girlfriend was out of town, her best friend gave me oral sex. Now I want to see both of them. Any advice?

Adam: You've got to get two penises. First off, that's not going to fly with the girlfriend. My theory with this kind of best friend stuff is the friend doesn't do it because you turn her on. The whole payoff is going to be her letting her friend find out. She didn't do it because she's so turned on by you; she did it because she wants to screw over her friend, ultimately. You start up with this girl, you guys are going to become involved and then she's going to start threatening to tell your girlfriend and it's going to be a disaster.

★ **Greg:** In his book, Marilyn Manson has a little thing of rules. On it, he says he doesn't think blow jobs are cheating. It's just like a handshake, he calls it.

Adam: Sure—but we've got to get women to sign off on that. I think all of us guys can get together and agree on that, but it's sort of like us agreeing that hot dogs are good for you without getting the medical community involved. I don't think we're ever going to get women to sign off on that one, that's what I'm saying.

Dr. Drew: Stay away from both of them is my advice. The friend is not a friend.

Adam: God bless women trying to get back at other women by blowing guys.

Dr. Drew: Especially this best friend thing.

Adam: It's a horrible impulse, but it ends up paying dividends for the guy. The thing that's funny about it is I know this chick is just screwed up enough to be pissed at her friend and probably won't even enter the guy into the mix. I see it on *Jerry Springer* all the time. Some guy who banged two women, sitting in between them while they are going at each other. Saying, "He loves me more."

Dr. Drew: This is a good argument for choosing a best friend very carefully. Whenever we hear about horribly chaotic relationships, they always seem to involve the best friend. I think people choose their best friend the way they choose a boyfriend. If they were abused, they choose an abusive boyfriend and an abusive best friend.

Q: I'm trying to talk my girlfriend into having a threesome. I'm kind of worried because I want to be sure we find someone who's clean. What should I do?

Dr. Drew: Don't do it. Usually this is somebody trying to talk his wife into it. Rather than try to find a partner, I suggest they try to find a divorce attorney because they are going to need that sooner.

He's worried because he wants to be sure to find someone clean. What are you going to do? Go into the clinic beforehand and get checked out?

Adam: You're really endangering the relationship with your girlfriend. Feelings are going to change. They are going to change in a big way.

Dr. Drew: It really destabilizes relationships. Feelings that come out of it are always surprising to people.

Adam: I think everyone, at nineteen, should do this, have it sabotage a relationship.

Dr. Drew: So you learn why not to do it.

Adam: So you get it over with and don't do it at twenty-three when you are married, before you have kids.

Q: How does engaging in three-way sex destabilize a relationship?

Adam: Look at it this way. If you're in a relationship and your wife says, "Hey, we should get another guy in here, and have sex with the three of us," or another girl—well, right there, what she's saying is that, whatever you are, it ain't enough. So the relationship is already suspect by virtue of the fact that you're going to the bullpen for a second penis. Now—is that going to somehow enhance the relationship and get it back on course? Or is it going to magnify problems in the relationship and stir it up more?

Dr. Drew: It's the feelings that come out of physical intimacy that our society doesn't tell people they get. When you bring a third person in, even if it's a prostitute, people develop feelings for people they're physically intimate with.

Adam: Oh, come on, Drew—if you and Susan brought a prostitute in, you wouldn't develop feelings for the prostitute and neither would Susan. Unless the prostitute was really hot. Then it would be all right.

But it wakes up a bunch of stuff—it unearths stuff in you and in your partner. And the intimacy between you and your partner—between you and Susan—is jeopardized.

Dr. Drew: She starts to get angry at you for enjoying sex with a prostitute.

Adam: Right. But it's not as if you want to leave with the hooker.

Dr. Drew: No, but that happens, too. A lot of unstable feelings come out.

Adam: It stirs things up inside of you and inside of your partner. It creates something—I don't think that they worry that you'll get attached to that third person, although that's certainly an option. It's mainly that it stirs up stuff between you.

Q: Is three-way sex something that only men fantasize about?

Dr. Drew: It's often initiated by a woman in an attempt to satisfy the guy. It's virtually never without a guy whispering it in her ear somewhere. The exception, I suppose, is the woman who is looking for a "safe" way to explore lesbian feelings.

Adam: Is it ever initiated by a woman who's not abused or who's not a little bit off? That's very rare.

Dr. Drew: Exceedingly rare. Unheard of.

Adam: It's heard of but—

Dr. Drew: Not in a stable relationship. If they're in college in a dorm or something, I could see it as part of experimentation. But if they're in a stable relationship, if they're thinking about getting married, no way. A woman who says, "Honey, I really want to bring a girl in, I think that would be cool," or "I want to bring another guy in"—that's somebody who's been abused at sometime in their life, almost without exception.

Adam: How do we know that? Because we do what the FBI does when they try to compile profiles of serial killers: It gets down to some kid has been molested and killed and they know it's a guy within a four-mile radius of the house and there's about a 90 percent probability of that. People are people; that's how it works.

That's the same thing we do with threesomes. Hey, I wish it did work out—I really do. But it just doesn't seem to. People have tried it a few times; they report back to us and it just doesn't seem to work out.

Q: Can promiscuity in your past hurt your chances of having a real relationship in the future?

Dr. Drew: Future partners could hold it against you.

Adam: Women don't normally hold it against men. Men more often hold it against women. There's an interesting scene in Woody Allen's movie *Mighty Aphrodite,* where the boyfriend finds out that the woman he's dating was in porn movies and basically freaks out—he hits her and dumps her and leaves. Then they fast-forward some years and she's married to a helicopter pilot who knew about her past but didn't mind it—even found it amusing. It really shows the two extremes of guys right there.

Dr. Drew: But there must have been dramatic change for her to be in a stable relationship with somebody like that. The human reality of somebody who is in porn movies is somebody who had real problems. And if you're going to try to be in a relationship with somebody like that, you're going to be able to do it only by addressing the reality and not by idealizing them.

By the same token, if you can't deal with somebody's past, well, we all have pasts. I wasn't born a doctor. You come to who you are through various paths. Some people's paths are very intense and dangerous and destructive.

Adam: The bottom line is: Some guys are very conservative about their partner's past. I speak from the male standpoint here. Women are a little more pragmatic because they're more concerned about the present. It will drift back in moments of insecurity, if guys talk about their old girlfriends. But women are much more into present performance than past performance.

Q: Why does this seem to be more of an issue for men than for women?

Dr. Drew: Guys have a thing about idealizing women. They've got to be pure and chaste. Men don't have to be.

Adam: Some guys are very concerned with it and some guys could really care less—because some guys are insecure and some aren't. I haven't been able to find a through-line with this; it doesn't have to do with being smart or being nice guys. It's just the way some guys are, like having a sense of humor or hand–eye coordination. I'm not sure why, but there it is: With some guys, it's a nonissue. With others, even the mention of her first boyfriend makes the guy want to go back and kill him.

Dr. Drew: People in our society are very threatened by female sexuality. Or, I should say, men are threatened by it; women aren't. But it points out how much women are asked to be either chaste or promiscuous. She can't be a total person who at one time in her life was promiscuous and at another time wasn't. Men hold it against them; society holds it against them.

Adam: Some do and some don't. I imagine someone like Madonna has had a ton of guys, a ton of relationships. But plenty of guys would be happy to get in with her.

It's also different for guys at different stages of their lives. Younger guys—nineteen or twenty years old—are very pumped up about this. It's very disturbing to them. I've seen myself go through this: Looking through some yearbook, seeing a picture of her old boyfriend, and being so disturbed by that image. Now, in my thirties, well, I don't look at it as maturity. It's more like losing the will—the fight's out of me. It's just sort of okay. You've been with a bunch of guys but you're not with them now. I'll just let it go. It's testosterone—an energy you had that you just don't have anymore.

Dr. Drew: Some of it is the idealized images we have of Mom and women in general. The other is being secure that she's a separate person—I'm okay by myself and I like this other person and I accept her for who she is.

Adam: However, our societal standards about promiscuity are undoubtedly based on some truth, in that people learn that people who have been with multiple partners could be dangerous or chaotic. I don't mind someone who's horny, someone who likes a little stimulation. That's good for twenty or

DR. DREW

on Promiscuity and Sexual Compulsion and Addiction

Sexual addiction tends to be part of the same biology as any other addiction. People require constant brain rewards, constant gratification, in spite of consequences. The true addict will have no concern about the consequences; he'll continue to pursue sex, even as the consequences mount.

There's compulsive sexual acting out, which is often a reaction to some traumatic event in the past—such as abuse. They try to use sex as a way of avoiding feelings, to the point that it becomes compulsive.

Gender differences have been observed in sexual compulsions. Men tend to engage in activities that treat women as objects; women tend to use sex to distort power—either to gain control over men or to heighten their own victimization.

They develop mounting problems and consequences from the sexual behavior, whether it's spending money, disrupting relationships or school or their jobs or their health. If that behavior can't be controlled, then it's a true sexual addiction. It usually responds very well to Sex Addicts Anonymous, or SAA, which will focus on management of important feelings that have an impact on their behavior, particularly feelings of aggression.

thirty partners. But it ain't good for one hundred and twenty or one hundred and thirty. That's acting out. There is no way you can rack up certain numbers without it being overt compensation. I don't like to see anyone with an agenda. And that is a man on a mission.

8

Infidelity

Celebrity Input

★ ***from Rapper-Actor Ice T***

★ ★ ★ **Q: One day I was over at my girlfriend's house and she wasn't home. Her mother started flirting with me. The next thing I knew we were having sex. Now her mom's always coming on to me but neither of us has told my girlfriend. How do I get rid of the mom and not spoil the relationship?**

Dr. Drew: The relationship's already spoiled. It's done. There are certain boundaries that, once you cross over, you just don't go on back. I would say this is one of them. You can't salvage a relationship that is so destroyed.

Adam: I always have a theory when this stuff goes down: that the mom and the daughter both have to be nuts. Because there is no way someone could have been raised in this house without being a little bit nuts. The acorn doesn't fall too far from the tree.

Dr. Drew: And the guy doesn't deserve the girl. If a guy will do that to her, the relationship is already so destroyed, it's just over. Maybe Ice T has a different idea.

★ **Ice T:** I've been in this situation where I've been on a blind date and walked into a house and the mother was lying there on the couch and I thought it was the girl I was supposed to be meeting. Because a lot of times, the mother might only be fifteen years older than the daughter. So I just saw her mother from the back and I was, like, "Okay!" And then she just kind of looked up and said the girl's name, she's in the bedroom. I'm like, "Oh, shit, your mother's fine." But, it didn't go any further than that. Her mother never started flirting with me.

Dr. Drew: What if the mom did come on to you?

★ **Ice T:** Well, now that's not cool at all. I mean, me personally, I would have brought it to the girl, you know. That would have been the way I would have handled it. I would have said to the girl, "Your mom's flirting with me. What's up with that?"

Adam: Don't you think it's a lot of guys' fantasies, though, to get the daughter and the hole she came out of?

Dr. Drew: You're talking about some sort of power play.

★ **Ice T:** Yeah.

Dr. Drew: It's just such a violation. Anybody who would need that kind of crazy power over people is not somebody that anyone should be involved with. That's somebody who also probably robs banks and things, too.

Adam: So what's our advice to this kid?

Dr. Drew: Cut your losses and start over somewhere else. Learn from this and don't violate boundaries that you shouldn't be violating.

★ **Ice T:** He already crossed the boundary. He should have never done it.

Adam: Now he's got to back off and get out of there, I think.

★ **Ice T:** Yeah—quick.

Q: Why do people cheat in a committed relationship?

Dr. Drew: Some people cheat in order to sustain intimacy because it's too frightening to be in a single relationship. If you're in a one-to-one relationship, you have to be vulnerable; you have to show yourself for who you are and share yourself in a real way.

If you're cheating, you're still deflecting things: "Yeah, I'm okay because I still have my attention and my emotions tied up over here. I'm not focusing on my fear of intimacy in my primary relationship. I have a way of distancing myself from my feelings a little bit," which is this other person you also don't care about. You get this sort of immediate, intense thing, some kind of lust acting out. But in comes the other relationship and you don't care about that person really either.

MYTHBUSTERS

Myth: *You're not cheating if you're not having sex with the person.*

The truth, according to Dr. Drew: This is hard for me to understand. Cheating is more in the heart than in the act itself. If you are violating another person's trust, you are cheating.

Adam: Cheating is done by insecure people who need to be propped up by others. This is the reason that cheaters cheat. And there's no satisfaction in cheating. It's not that you need that person or you need someone else. Cheating is a disease.

Dr. Drew: We'll commonly hear, "Oh, I was bored with my wife. Our sex life was boring so I had to go do this thing." Which means, "It no longer kept me distanced from my feelings, didn't prop me up the way I needed to be propped up, so I had to go act on it." God forbid you should have a real feeling.

Q: Are there degrees of cheating?

Adam: You either cheat or you don't. I think the cruelest thing you can do to a partner is to cheat with someone uglier than they are. Men: Never cheat with someone who's fatter than your wife. That's the ultimate insult, the ultimate slap in the face. It's really weird or bizarre, but I've spoken to women who've been cheated on and I swear to you that's a factor. When they perceive that the other woman is ugly or overweight or less physically appealing, it makes it twice as bad.

Dr. Drew: It's like somehow women have a scale of justice, that they could understand if it was someone more attractive.

Adam: It's such a competitive, physical game out there. Good-looking women are in such demand—and they're praised by other women as much as anything. Women are really into Cindy Crawford: "Oh, she's beautiful, she's so smart, so wonderful. Look at the life she's forging." That's why all these women's magazines have her on the cover. It's chicks reading about chicks. Whereas guys don't give a shit about Brad Pitt. Guys could give a rat's ass what Mel Gibson is up to.

Dr. Drew: Women are so used to dealing with male biology that they could almost understand, if a woman was terribly attractive.

Q: What if you're actually having a relationship problem?

Dr. Drew: Then the cheating is a symptom of that, as opposed to an internal problem.

Adam: But it's still a cowardly act.

Q: How can you tell if someone is cheating?

Adam: If you're the kind of person who's in tune with what's going on, you'll know.

Dr. Drew: You should know beforehand, when you're at risk for that to happen.

Adam: A guy, if his eyes are open, should see the signs—although he probably doesn't have his eyes open. He's not paying enough attention and that's why she's cheating. Women build into an affair. Men can just go do it: He can ask a woman to marry him, get engaged, be flying home that night to tell his parents, and meet the stewardess and, you know, pow! A woman would never do that.

Q: Are there telltale signs?

Adam: I think guys are a little easier to read. It's just overcompensation.

Dr. Drew: If a guy is bringing home flowers and buying her things, wanting to have more sex, there's a tip-off.

Adam: I would say, also, if he's taking an unusual interest in his own appearance: buying himself a new sports coat or going to the gym a little more.

Dr. Drew: Unusual or uncomfortable behavior: If you notice you're not comfortable with what the other person is telling you about his plans and find yourself saying things like "Where are you going? How does that work? Why are you doing that?" you should listen to yourself. Don't deny that something is going on. When something is up, something is up. That's all there is to it.

Q: Don't people give themselves away in other ways?

Adam: I would almost say that anyone who gets caught, it's because there's an element of wanting to get caught. I don't know if it's stupidity or wanting to get caught—or if wanting to be caught means you're stupid. Most men get caught cheating not because a surveillance camera was installed in the nightstand and not because she hired a private eye but because he just basically left some irrefutable evidence in plain view. He's getting undressed at night and he's wearing the wrong underwear. Or she finds love notes or messages on the Internet, or in the glove compartment of the family car, or in his pocket when she's doing the laundry.

I don't believe a woman who is cheating is going to tip her hand that way. What she's going to do is get drunk and yell it at you. You won't know a damn thing is going on—and that's part of it, too.

Dr. Drew: Exactly. That's the reason she's cheating. Because you don't even pay enough attention to her to know that she was cheating.

Adam: So you'll get into a little argument and she's a little loaded. And you tell her you're tired of her nagging—and she yells it at you. She wants to drop it in your lap: "Look what you made me do. See what happens when you don't pay attention to me?"

Q: The old saying goes, "Confession is good for the soul." Is that true when you've been cheating?

Adam: There are two reasons I believe people tell their partners. First, because they feel they need to tell the truth. Well, I don't trust people who do that.

"I felt they needed to know." When I hear somebody say that, it's like when I hear people say, "I'm suing, but it's not for the money." It ranks right up there with, "I'd like to help, but . . ." No, you wouldn't like to help because as soon as you hear the phrase, "I'd like to help," it means you'll get no help. As soon as you hear the phrase, "I'm suing but it's not about money," it's always about the money. And the same with the truth. People tell people the truth to alleviate their own guilt, that's number one.

And number two, they confess in order to act out some aggression. That's at the heart of it all: to let the other person know what you're capable of doing. "Hey, look, other people appreciate me even if you don't." It's a little bit of an "F— you."

As God is my witness, if my wife cheated on me—just a one-time indiscretion kind of thing—I really wouldn't want to know. I'd be more angry if she told me.

Q: Is there a difference in the reasons men and women cheat?

Adam: It's in a man's biology to have multiple partners. When you take that man and his biology and you ship his ass to Philadelphia while the wife and kids are back in L.A.—and then you put a little beer in that biology and mix in a secretary who's at the firm in Philadelphia who's also having a few beers at the social after the business meeting—obviously things can happen. To me, that's biology meets circumstances. Biology meets opportunity.

Dr. Drew: But it also needs momentum. Women on the other hand tend to do that stuff as a response to their own problems, as opposed to biology, which happens less occasionally.

Adam: That's right. When a man cheats, it's not necessarily because there's a relationship problem. But when a woman cheats, you've got a problem.

Dr. Drew: If a woman cheats, it's usually got to be an emotional shortcoming in the relationship. It may be something as simple as not spending enough time and attention on that person. Women have the equivalent of a gas tank, which has to be filled with a certain amount of this attention and giving. If they don't get it, then they act out the biology.

Adam: Yes, they go looking for a pump when the tank goes dry. Women cheat because they're missing something in their relationship—or to even the score. The guy goes on autopilot and the woman wants attention. You don't have to connect too many dots to figure out that, if you weren't coming home drunk and passing out on the sofa for the last six months straight and not paying them any kind of attention—it's: "Stop me before I cheat again." What's the saying? "A new broom sweeps clean"? Yes, and a new man cuddles often.

Q: What about the difference between the way the two sexes respond to temptation?

Adam: Put it this way: As a man, how much experience do you have turning women down? Women, by the time they're twenty-four, twenty-five, they've been around, been to a bar or two in their lives—and they're well-equipped to say no. You'll hear women talking all the time, even women who aren't in relationships: "This guy came up and he was talking to me. He was kind of cute. Did I

ADAM on More Differences Between the Way Men and Women View Cheating

Why do guys cheat? Because they can. Guys cheat because it's in their nature.

Women cheat because they're missing something in their relationship.

For a guy, it's okay for his woman to have a male friend as long as there's no sexual history between them. It takes some of the pressure off the relationship. Guys have no problem with a woman talking to another man. They'd rather she talk to him all the time than give a guy a hand job in the parking lot one time.

A woman would rather that her man get laid on a business trip than have some attractive woman at the office he can discuss philosophy with. To a woman, it's not okay for a guy to have a woman friend.

If a woman initiates sex, it helps a guy rationalize cheating in his own mind. It's like the difference between finding money in the street and knocking over a liquor store.

give him my number? No, I thought he was kind of a jerk."

Imagine that same conversation with a single man—or even a married man—and an attractive woman comes up to him in a bar offering to buy him a drink. "No thanks"? I don't think so. You never hear that.

And let's face it: The whole reason a lot of guys try to make the good living—to drive the nice car and wear the Armani suit—is to get the woman. So when a woman does the asking, guys aren't used to saying no.

★ ***from Actor French Stewart***

Q: I think my wife is cheating on me. I haven't actually caught her but I have a lot of suspicions and a lot of circumstantial evidence. What should I do? I don't want to do anything that will upset our little girl too much.

Dr. Drew: I think you trust your instincts. At the very least, you know there is something very wrong in your relationship. As part of your commitment to your little girl, in addition to keeping the environment stable and relatively chaos-free, you get some professional help. You let your wife know that you love and care about her and that you want things to survive. You want the relationship to continue and you really think you should consider some professional help to keep things together.

★ **French:** Wow. God, I would just say, ask her. I think you've got to ask her. If you start trying to second-guess whether she is or isn't and reacting that way, it could turn out that you are just a hothead and you don't know what you are talking about. So I think you just have to ask her.

Adam: I'm just playing devil's advocate here. Obviously she's going to lie. And then you are back at square one—except she knows you think something's up. Which may make her less vulnerable to detection. But I don't know what the alternative is other than dust her panties for fingerprints or hire a detective or something.

★ **French:** But I think this question hinges purely on what kind of person you are. I know people who think things are going on with their companions and they're just hotheads. They're just suspicious people.

Adam: Right. There are people who have genuine reasons to be suspicious and then there are those who thought every person they've ever been involved in a relationship with cheated on them.

But how about this approach, French? All you do is you pick out the name of, let's say, your wife's best friend. We'll make up a name, we'll call her Connie. You say, "Listen, I spoke to Connie the other night. She had a few beers, she almost broke down crying, but she told me the whole sordid truth about you carrying on." Now, if the woman really is cheating, you'll hear her yell, "I'll kill that bitch," or "He didn't mean a thing to me."

I admit, it's a little manipulative. But in every relationship, once every three months, I will say, "I heard what you said to Connie about me," just waiting for them to crack.

★ **French:** Is it always Connie?

Adam: Always Connie, even if they don't know a Connie. Connie will still work. But I'm with you, French. I think you should ask them straight out. Then realize that if they don't come clean, there is no second asking after that. And if, in fact, they are cheating and they are lying, they are going to be extra careful now. But maybe they lie when you ask—and then they call their lover and say it's over. You're none the worse for wear, except if you got crabs.

Q: If you find out a partner has been cheating, should you stay or should you go?

Adam: You have to decide two things: Is this person likely to do it again? And am I going to hold it against this person? If the answer is yes to either one of those questions, you can't get back together. If they're going to cheat or you suspect they're going to cheat, you can't get back together. If you can't forgive them and will never stop holding this against them, you can't get together.

Dr. Drew: If you can't trust them, you can't reestablish the relationship because you're not going to be open to them.

Look at your own family system. If you come from a system where cheating is accepted, get some treatment because it's not going to stop. That model is emblazoned in your head: that men can just behave that way. But that's not the way guys should be. It's the way women allow them to be.

If a person is clear that it was an absolute, categorical mistake, that it was some kind of extraordinary circumstance, and if forgiveness is possible, then the relationship can probably move forward on a basis of honesty. In an ideal relationship, it's better for all the information to be available. There's a saying in Alcoholics Anonymous: "You're as sick as your secrets." The more an individual hides who he is, the less truth there is. For a relationship to be healthy, there needs to be as much truth as possible about who these people are in the relationship for the relationship to be genuine and real. Yes, it's painful to deal with the truth—but that's the road to health.

★ *from Writer-Director-Performer Keenen Ivory Wayans*

Q: I'm happily married but I also want to have a threesome. I've just about convinced my wife. How do we find a partner?

Dr. Drew: Find a divorce attorney; don't worry about your partner. This is probably two people who never had an intimate relationship and they are satisfied to get a stable situation together. Of course, they have to sabotage that and create a little drama. They'll do that if they get a threesome.

Adam: People don't buy into that concept of sabotage. But try thinking of it this way:

The relationship becomes like something on the potter's wheel where it's spinning around, perfectly centered. And you knock it out and before you know it's wobbling out of control and flying off.

★ **Keenen:** Let his wife do the hunting. Let it be somebody she's comfortable with, somebody that she's not going to be threatened by and somebody she's not going to feel that he's already slept with.

Adam: Do you think it's a good idea, Keenen, for it to be a stranger?

★ **Keenen:** Yeah.

Adam: I would, too.

★ **Keenen:** I think it should be not only just a stranger, but somebody you don't expect to see again.

Adam: It seems to me that the safest way to go about this, in terms of not jeopardizing your relationship, is calling in a professional.

★ **Keenen:** I tend to agree. I mean, I personally am not into the whole working-girl thing. I do think, in this particular case, that someone who will come in and do the job and leave is probably your best bet. If it's not a woman's idea to have the threesome, then you are walking on a line of really ruining your relationship.

Adam: Women will let you talk them into things temporarily and you may think you are getting away with it, but it will come back to haunt you.

★ **Keenen:** Absolutely.

Adam: It could be five years down the road. They'll let you know in other ways that aren't so subtle that this was a bad idea and you should have listened to them when they told you they didn't want to do it in the first place.

★ **Keenen:** A lot of times, guys are opening up a can of worms, and they have no idea what's inside. Even for themselves: Now that they've done this, if they like it, they're going to want to do it again. God help you if you ever twist your mouth after she's already gone and done it for you, to ask her to do it again. That's why I said I just think it's a bad idea.

Adam: What are your options? Either you both hate it, in which case what good did it do you? Or you love it—and now you are screwed.

★ **Keenen:** That's right. Now you are hooked on something that you're just not going to be able to get.

Dr. Drew: It's not realistic to say that a threesome doesn't sound good to every man. If it's with two women, it sounds good.

But you have a choice. Remember that. You have a choice.

I have three kids. I love my wife. I would never do that no matter how good it sounded, in order to preserve their happiness and the stability of our system.

Q: How do you personally deal with the idea of cheating?

Dr. Drew: My feeling about cheating has evolved to a different level, because I'm married and have kids. Although I still have impulses toward other women, the thought of acting on it is such a hostile act toward my wife, such a horrible act directly toward her and my children, that's it's unthinkable, no matter how profound the circumstances or the potential. To have such a lack of respect or empathy for someone with whom your life is so closely shared—I don't even get it.

Adam: Yeah, but wait a minute. What if you were out promoting this book and we were in Canada . . .

Dr. Drew: . . . and there was no way to get caught . . .

Adam: I'm not trying to talk you into it. What I'm saying is, you like women—you probably like women more than I do. You admire women. You like to look at women. Your package is a little more sterile than mine but the innards are just as putrid, believe me, or worse.

So we're in Canada and a very beautiful Canadian woman approaches you and we've been on the road for two weeks solid—and a man has needs. She wants, let's say, to give you oral pleasure in a limo. Now why is that an attack against Susan and the kids? I mean, I know you wouldn't want Susan screwing around with the gardener while you're gone—but all you've done is relieve a little pressure. You go back to Pasadena and it doesn't lessen the love you have for her and your kids. Why is that such an attack?

Dr. Drew: It's a symbolic attack and I couldn't bring myself to do it. I couldn't. I couldn't live with myself. Not because I wouldn't want to get caught. It just feels so horrible to me.

9

Internet Sex

Q: How is the Internet as a place to meet people?

Dr. Drew: Pathetic. There's no real relationship there.

Q: Is it any worse than answering a personal ad or going to a video dating service?

Dr. Drew: At least those are attempts to measure people against one another; those are potential relationships. If you meet through a personal ad or a video dating service, there's more of a representation of a person there: a person you can see, feel, touch, know. When we actually meet a person, we can learn things about them just from the way they look, their body language, the way they sound and just our gut reaction—the kind of visual and biological cues we've learned to interpret from the time we were infants.

Adam: It's almost the best part of a relationship. But the Internet is pure fantasy: It's like the party before the Super Bowl, when you're sure your team is going to win. Not in the fourth quarter when you're down by seventeen points and you drank too much and ate too many corn dogs. That's the beauty of a Super Bowl party: There are thirty guys all rooting for another team but they're all sitting there and they're all so sure everything is going to work out and it feels so good.

Dr. Drew: But with the Internet, it's all fantasy. There's no person there.

Adam: I think that's what attracts a lot of people. They say, "Well, I don't do so well out at the club scene." What they're saying is, "I don't like the reality part of relationships. I like this part." And the reason they don't do so well is because they can't handle the part of the relationship where there's—

Dr. Drew: —risk, vulnerability. On the Internet, people are developing something they call a relationship before the two people actually meet. And that is pure fantasy.

It shows how much these relationships are about projecting your own needs on other people. Because there's no person there. You have no concept of who the person is; there's just a little bit of interplay on certain issues and the rest of it is created in the imagination. It's less of a relationship than we have with people on the radio.

If the two people actually meet, there's already a fantasy, an idealization that so clouds the reality that it's very difficult for any real relationship to develop.

★ from Rocker Kevin Coleman of Smashmouth

★ ★ ★ **Q: I've been meeting someone online in a chat room for a couple of months and we really hit it off. I'm an eighteen-year-old girl and he says he's twenty-two. He lives in the next state and now he wants to come visit me. We've gotten pretty steamy in our online chats but I'm worried that he might expect sex if we meet in person. I'm not sure I'm ready for that. What should I do?**

Dr. Drew: So he wants to meet her and she thinks he's expecting more than she's willing to give.

Adam: Listen guys, online for women can be a full meal, with a beginning, middle, and end. For guys it's an appetizer. We're waiting for the main course.

Dr. Drew: It's not even an appetizer. It's fishing.

Adam: Yeah. It's just chum, just a little blood in the water.

Dr. Drew: For women, it's a Harlequin novel.

Adam: Yeah, it can be a whole relationship for them. For guys, the whole point is to finish the job. Get some payday in there.

★ **Kevin:** I had an experience with a dating service. My experience with anything like that is just leave it to the computer. There are better ways of meeting people, believe me. I just don't think that you should go.

Adam: It's all about her safety.

★ **Kevin:** People don't talk normally on a computer. From my experience, believe me, I would just steer clear. I had a bad experience with just a total headcase girl. I mean she was really, really hot, but she's was a fucking nutcase.

Adam: But she was hot?

★ **Kevin:** Super-hot.

Adam: You met a super-hot chick over the computer?

★ **Kevin:** Right.

Adam: That destroys a lot of theories I had.

★ **Kevin:** But she was a headcase. I mean a stalker.

Adam: All right, so the moral of the story is, "Buyer beware."

★ **Kevin:** Absolutely, you might end up in a body bag somewhere.

Adam: Relationships take a little work. I always think there is something wrong with somebody who thinks they can find one on the Internet.

Dr. Drew: To go so far as to fly a distance and meet with somebody with whom you can never really maintain a real relationship anyway because of proximity issues, I have grave concerns about that. The men who engage in this typically are looking for people who have difficulty functioning socially anyway. My big message to people is: Deal in reality, folks.

★ **Kevin:** Everything that you are experiencing online is a fantasy formulated in your head. It's not based on reality. You know what I mean? It's the fantasy you create in your own head instead of having something tangible. That's why people hide behind the computer.

Adam: It's, like, you want a good body, you've got to go to the gym. You've got to work out. You can't buy one of those electronic pulse machines and strap it to your ass. This is the same thing. There is no easy way to get around this.

Dr. Drew: This is a case in point of why we disdain online relationships: because they are all built on fantasy and there is no person, no human element to this. It's all based on nonsense. When you come to meet face-to-face, you have all of those fantasies superimposed on the relationship and it never comes down to reality. We would strongly urge against it here, because they live too far apart. It's not a real relationship. Certainly she shouldn't do anything she doesn't want to do.

Q: Do these relationships ever work out?

Dr. Drew: The question should be: How often do you hear about them being terribly disappointing? We rarely hear about successful relationships. They may happen but we rarely hear about them. The norm at this point on the Internet is to have these lengthy relationships across the computer before there is even phone contact. Already they're involved in something that's not real and not right.

Adam: Internet sex is a great metaphor for life. It's like saying, "Should I work my ass off and work my way up through the ranks—or should I just go buy a Lotto ticket and hope I hit it?" It's the path of least resistance—and people tend to do what's easiest.

Q: What can you assume about somebody you meet there?

Adam: That the seventeen-year-old cheerleader you think you're talking to may actually be a forty-five-year-old Merchant Marine.

Dr. Drew: That they're not who they say they are. Whatever it is, people idealize themselves and others constantly.

Adam: There's a reason why people are sitting in front of their computers, instead of going out meeting people. Maybe it's because you're a pedophile who doesn't want to be known. Maybe there's something very physically apparent wrong with you—like you're a guy instead of the woman you claim to be. Or you're saying you're a bikini model and you weigh two hundred fifty pounds.

Or maybe there's an emotional reason: You have difficulty communicating with other people on a one-to-one basis. Personally, I'd rather take my chances on the emotional stuff and work my way through it. The key to life is this: You've got to take your lumps.

Q: Are there actual dangers to creating personal relationships via the Internet?

Dr. Drew: I know that kids get involved in inappropriate interactions with older people online. They're usually dragged into an inappropriate interaction by abusive individuals. We read about this in the paper every day: young people being sexually abused by much older adults they've met online, adults who pretend to be other young people, who then lure them into meetings and end up molesting them.

I'm generally concerned about young people interacting in an overtly sexual way before the age of sixteen, definitely before the age of fourteen. It's really abusive—or bordering on abuse—under the age of twelve. The kind of overt sexual overtones that are routinely part of some of these online chat rooms can be damaging to kids. They don't have the neurological development or the maturity to assess what this information is. It can be overwhelming to them, and potentially quite damaging.

10

Overdependency

Celebrity Input

★ ***from Steve Harwell of Smashmouth***

★ ★ ★ **Q: I met a girl I like a lot and started having sex and going out. I like her but it's not like I'm going to marry her. But she's already trying to convince me to move in together and seems to spend every spare minute at my place. She's even redecorating my apartment. I'm flattered but she's going too fast. How do I slow her down?**

Dr. Drew: Be honest. Women have an amazing way of assuming that, if you are sexually active with them and they are having a delightful intimate experience with you, that you are sharing that experience. For men, of course, it may be something quite different.

★ **Steve:** How do you slow her down? You leave a number of another girl where she's going to find it.

Adam: Oh, so you trip her up and piss her off at the same time.

Dr. Drew: Why would you choose a route that would be potentially very painful to the woman? Why not just step forward and be honest? It's certainly a cowardly way out. This thing is going to get worse with time. So better you should face the music now.

★ **Steve:** No, what you say is, "You know what? You moved in too quick, you got too personal with my shit—now look what happened. You stumbled across something I didn't want you to see. I can't help it."

Adam: Don't you think that may cut things off altogether?

★ **Steve:** No, because if she's that serious about moving in, and that serious about making this thing go quicker than it should go, she's not going to trip. She'll trip for like a day and then she'll be, like, "Okay, maybe I was too intense on this. Maybe I should back off a little bit and give things a chance to evolve instead of already picking out curtains."

Adam: You think she's not going to trust you from that point on?

★ **Steve:** She just found a number that maybe was there from six months ago, a year ago. But I let her see that I haven't cleared my space yet. You know what I'm saying?

Adam: That's pretty solid. I'm with you on this one.

★ **Steve:** I haven't cleared my space enough to where she can just come dive in and act like everything's all cool. I had my own life before this, and all of a sudden you just move in and invade my whole space? Maybe I wasn't ready. So I've got to make it look like, you know what? I haven't cleared out my closet yet, before you can just move your stuff in. Because you know what? Puppy love ends real quick when you live together.

Dr. Drew: I think he should just be honest. Tell her it's too fast.

Adam: This is a tricky conversation to have. I don't know if you have a real sit-down or if you can slowly dissuade them—

Dr. Drew: —by not being available so much.

Adam: There are a couple of little subtleties you should know. If they are talking about coming over and spending the night, you should be talking about having to get up pretty early the next day with some sort of presentation.

Dr. Drew: But it's not all about the girl. The guy didn't have to let her in. It can be hard sometimes to prevent intrusions, but start asserting yourself. We would tell a girl the same thing about a guy who was coming on too fast sexually. Just assert yourself clearly.

Adam: But you can assert it through your actions without a real sit-down, meltdown, breakdown conversation.

Dr. Drew: I think eventually it comes down to that conversation, though. Somehow you get there eventually. And people who allow intrusions usually were parented by people who are very intrusive and didn't allow an autonomous development of the individual.

Adam: Ultimately, she's doing herself a favor by not putting the screws to this guy. Because when it comes to commitment and long-term relationships, guys are like trying to get a cat into the box that you take it to the vet with. The trick is not to chase it around the house with a beach towel. Instead, put some food in the cage, put the cage in the living room, and walk away.

Q: What are some of the symptoms of overdependency?

Dr. Drew: Anytime you need somebody in order to be complete, you're overdependent. Anytime you get in a situation where you lose yourself in a relationship, you're too dependent. If you're in a situation where you can't get out because there's something about what that person has that you can't do without, you're in trouble.

To the extent that your feelings become another person's, that's too much. On the other hand, to be overly independent with no concern for the feelings of others is not right either; that heads toward a narcissistic relationship.

You should be independent. You should be a separate person who comes together in a relationship, not one who blends into a relationship. It's not like a puzzle where two pieces have to be together in order to fit or to complete one another. It's more two separate entities creating a new entity when they're together.

Adam: Right. You should be Neapolitan, not Rocky Road—not some sort of peanut butter–fudge swirl thing. Your goose is cooked the day you start thinking that there's no other like this person.

Dr. Drew: That's very dangerous. That's a fantasy.

Q: Where do you draw the line between a healthy relationship and overdependency?

Dr. Drew: Very difficult. Where are you enmeshed and where are you just connected? There have to be two separate entities who have mutuality and respect for each other.

Q: What age group is most susceptible to this?

Dr. Drew: The teens are when you get overenmeshed. But those relationships are largely based on fantasies from childhood.

Adam: All young relationships are overenmeshed. Even with your friends: You think you and your buddies are going to move to Hawaii and start some kind of outrigger business. It never turns out that way but you have this idea.

Dr. Drew: Everything is idealized. A lot of dependency is built on idealizations of people.

Adam: I can remember having those thoughts very vividly: *If I can never be with this particular person again, my God, I can't deal with that.*

Dr. Drew: That's a direct spin-off from Mommy, who left me, and I can't live without her.

Adam: Whether you're talking about a job or a relationship, you need the freedom to be yourself and be by yourself. That pressure of *I can't live without this* is a huge mistake. That's what you tend to get into when you're seventeen.

Q: How does overdependence relate to self-esteem?

Dr. Drew: It has to do with it, although I'm not sure it's purely self-esteem. It's not that common an issue, except in the context of what would be called code-

DR. DREW

How to Tell You're in an Enmeshed Relationship—and How to Get Out

Overdependent or enmeshed relationships are very common today: relationships in which there are poor boundaries, where people have difficulty determining what are their feelings and what are the other person's feelings. There's very little independence or respect for one another, no mutuality—just this overwhelming sense of fusion of the two individuals. And that can be very unhealthy—but also very common in people who have been in abusive families.

People who tend to find enmeshed relationships do so because their instincts—which have been skewed by the abuse in their past—direct them toward individuals with similar needs, people who tend to push the same emotional buttons, massage the same emotional needs.

A good sign that you're enmeshed to an unhealthy extent in a relationship is that other people—your friends, your family—are telling you that this relationship isn't good for you and yet you continue in it anyway. Or you're saying to yourself, *I know he's not good for me. I know this is not working.* Yet you continue to behave in a way that you can't control. If you're struggling to make the other person fit an idealized notion you have for them—then you're probably involved with the wrong person.

How do you get out? Well, as painful as it is, you have to stop denying the truth and confront it. And learn to deal with it, no matter how difficult that is. And that includes the truth about your own past of abuse.

Start by compelling your partner to behave in a way that's respectful of your needs. If they can't, extricate yourself from the situation—and find someone who is willing to respect your needs.

But that isn't easy. Telling the truth to yourself never is. So you should consider therapy to deal with the problems from your past that are infringing on your present efforts to be happy and fulfilled.

pendence. Most codependency is really closet narcissism by the kind of people who need to idealize the world and be idealized by the world so they can feel good about themselves. Their sense of self is poor and they need other people to prop them up. Yet they try to idealize their sense of the other person to prop him up. Fixing him is a way to feel good about themselves.

Adam: It's that balance between being removed and clinging to the relationship.

Dr. Drew: Clinginess is a part of dependency.

Q: How does it relate to addiction?

Dr. Drew: There are a lot of codependents who are addicts, and they use relationships as a way of not dealing with their own issues. They focus on other people's issues so they don't have to deal with the more painful reality of their own addiction.

Q: What if the other person doesn't mind how dependent you are?

Dr. Drew: Some people thrive on it.

Adam: But somewhere there's going to be a problem in a relationship built on that kind of dependency.

Dr. Drew: The person who is overdependent is going to feel more and more empty, less and less gratified, more and more angry than the person who thrives on dependencies to feel self-important. They feel less and less respectful of the person they're dependent upon. Eventually conflict will come up.

Q: Can this kind of relationship trigger depression when it ends?

Dr. Drew: Interestingly, both of us had depression triggered by clingy relationships, where we clung to people as a way of trying to make them something we needed them to be.

Adam: I didn't really cling while I was in the relationship. That was part of my problem.

Dr. Drew: No, but I did. That's why it lasted years and years, when it should have lasted five minutes. I'm the kind of person who tends to idealize others—or

I was at that point in my life. If they weren't fitting my idealized image, it shattered my life. If they then left, I had to deal with abandonment, too. I couldn't cope and I got depressed. So that poor young lady I was with at the time got clung to like I was some kind of pilot fish, a sucker fish just clinging to her. And it was all an attempt to avoid depression and avoid reality.

Adam: You weren't getting in touch with things you didn't want to get in touch with.

Dr. Drew: I was already depressed. But that clinging relationship kept me out of the depression phase. It kept me acting out upon her. Because I already had issues of loss and abandonment and lack of self-worth that were so intense. I think I was depressed by the age of nine. And everything beyond that was trying to manage depression.

And I was clinging to this girl, clinging to prevent depression, to try to hang on to something, like a life preserver.

Young Drew: *I'm nineteen and I want to know why nice guys always end up getting screwed in relationships. I've been so nice to women and I finally got a relationship and I just cherish her and she keeps doing things to me I can't believe.*

Adam: *You're hiding behind the words here. Let's replace "nice" with "needy."*

Young Drew: *I don't know that I'm needy.*

Adam: *Okay—how about clingy? Or insecure?*

Young Drew: *Well, I am kind of insecure. It's just that I'm having difficulty deciding what to do with my life. I'm in college and I'm having difficulty sleeping. I guess I'm depressed. I can't meet anybody and this girl that I've been with for a long time is seeing another guy now.*

Adam: *Are you done with her?*

Young Drew: *She's seeing another guy. That's the end of it, I guess.*

Adam: *Have you broken up?*

Young Drew: *I guess so.*

Adam: *She's seeing another guy. Why don't you break up with her for good?*

Young Drew: *I can't do that.*

Adam: *Doesn't it piss you off?*

Young Drew: *It pisses me off. It makes me really sad. But if I broke up—well, I came back to California from college in New England to be closer to her. I was depressed out there and now I'm really depressed. I don't know what to do with my life at this point.*

Dr. Drew: *Look, you've got to start dealing in reality here. You're floundering. It's obvious that you're depressed. If you're really smart, you ought to get some treatment for that, so you begin to get some clarity in what you need as a separate person. The relationship you're in right now is not a healthy one. If it's not over now, it should be over and you should end it. This person has mistreated you, probably because you cling so much that she has no other way out.*

Adam: *Has she tried to break up with you?*

Young Drew: *I guess so, over the years. She's giving me those messages now. But we've been together so long, our lives are so much a part of one another that I just can't see how she can imagine being away. I certainly can't imagine being without her.*

HOW TO HELP A FRIEND... *who is in an overdependent relationship*

Adam: It's really the same caveat you use with someone who's too promiscuous: Get this person to get involved with other aspects of their life and not shift it onto the person they're being dependent on. Show me a busy, successful, productive person and I'll show you someone who is not clingy.

Dr. Drew: That can sometimes be a compensation for somebody who was clingy at one time in their life and they become overachieving as a way of compensating for that. Clinginess is about not feeling worthwhile and not dealing with reality on reality's terms. So talk to them about dealing with reality on reality's terms. Don't try to make reality something it isn't.

11

When to Break Up, and How

Celebrity Input

★ *from Actor Jon Cryer*

★ ★ ★ **Q: I broke up with my boyfriend because I heard he had been fooling around. Now it turns out that it was a lie. How do I get him back?**

Dr. Drew: Let's sort of evaluate whether this relationship is worthy of rekindling. If it was so flimsy that the slightest threat would cause her to reject the guy, I've got to wonder. If you were the guy, Jon, would you come back to somebody who treated you like this?

★ **Jon:** Not if she didn't trust me enough to believe me in the first place when I said it was a lie.

ADAM Breakup Lines

- Tell him that all your friends hate him.
- Better yet, tell him that your parents hate him.
- "You're not going anywhere. You're a loser who's not going to amount to anything." Either he'll be motivated to turn himself into Donald Trump—or he'll jump off the nearest bridge.
- Chalk it up to physicality: "That ass is a deal-breaker." Or: "He's got a bigger penis than you."
- "I just need space." That's fine until you find out she's dating your buddy the next week. At which point you figure out it means, "I need space from you."
- "I've realized I'm gay." Tough to argue with—but it can be a double-edged sword when the word gets around.

The bottom line: As much bullshit as a person will buy is totally acceptable. If you can fake your own death, so be it. But it's got to be ironclad.

Dr. Drew: What could she have done to get you back? Think about it.

★ **Jon:** She would have to start a prolonged campaign, not unlike the Normandy invasion, basically. She would have to start with a singing telegram to soften me up. And then flowers.

Dr. Drew: I wouldn't think that coming back and saying, "Hey, I'm sorry, take me back," is a realistic approach. This is something that she's going to have to commit herself to and anticipate defeat. I mean anticipate that it may not be reality. She has to be more empathic in how she deals with her partners in the future.

★ **Jon:** That's the thing. If she believed the first rumor she heard about him messing around, then she doesn't trust him to begin with. So she's got to look at that.

Adam: If the guy is really into you, he'll come back. Although let's make an argument for you being just a little bit nutty. Unless there is some sort of very extreme circumstance, but I don't know then how you found out it was a lie.

Dr. Drew: You just be as apologetic as you can and you just find out if he's available. And if he's not, that's the consequence you get for behaving so rashly.

Q: Is there ever a right time to break up?

Dr. Drew: If there are kids involved, do your best to make it work. I'm not saying that two fighting parents are better than one, but to the extent that Mom has a terrible relationship with Dad, she's going to find some terrible people to bring to the house next—and Dad, too.

Q: What about if you're single and in your teens or twenties?

Dr. Drew: The saber and the clean cut—the swiftest, most direct way possible is the best. I think people should have the guts to do it face-to-face. It's very easy to write a letter or make a phone call. But have the courage and the respect to do it in person.

Q: What's the worst way to do it?

Adam: Try and get her to break up with you.

Dr. Drew: Sure, that's the fantasy of everyone who needs to break up.

Adam: That's a long, drawn-out, and painful process. By the time she gets to the breaking point, you've probably logged months of misery.

Dr. Drew: And really hurt the person. That's the thing: You end up hurting somebody more, as opposed to letting them begin to grieve their loss.

Adam: What could be worse than being forced to break up with somebody you don't want to break up with?

Dr. Drew: And they're doing it because of your behavior. Because you hurt them so much they have no choice.

Adam: That's horrible. I used to do that. I think I was probably frightened of the intimacy aspects. So I'd sabotage the relationship. But it would backfire because I'd get dragged back into it.

It was like I had this plan where I was going to sneak into Hitler's bunker, light the bomb, and then make a run for it. But the problem was I would slam the door behind me—and now it's me and Hitler locked in there and I couldn't deactivate the bomb. Hitler would be smart enough to get behind the cot and I'd actually be sitting on the bomb when it exploded.

Because I would get very deeply involved in the relationship. Then about six to eight months into it, I'd go on autopilot and start repelling the person and distancing myself from her—essentially forcing her to break up with me. Then, when she broke up with me, I would crumble like a spun-sugar stunt bottle—and I'd become singularly focused on getting that relationship back, probably in an attempt to repeat the process. And let me tell you, that kind of stuff pisses people off.

Dr. Drew: Forcing the other person to break up with you is even more cowardly than a letter.

Adam: I wouldn't even call it cowardly. It's just more screwed-up.

Dr. Drew: A lot of stuff that we talk about boils down to courage and cowardice. You have to have the courage to deal with the pain of challenging and confronting life on life's terms, as opposed to the cowardly route of delaying the pain.

How do you give somebody courage? How do you get somebody to hang in with painful material? You know how you do it and I know how you do it. You have to have very supportive, connected relationships with people important to you, such as your family. If you don't have that, it's almost intolerable for a human to step up and deal with the pain of something like a breakup.

Adam: Good point. We don't really use *coward* and *courage* anymore. They have almost been eliminated from our vocabulary. But that's ultimately what a lot of this is about.

Q: My girlfriend broke up with me because she said I was too jealous. She's willing to give me one more chance. I go nuts even if I see her talking to another guy. How do I deal with all this jealousy?

Dr. Drew: If you care enough about the other person, it's hard to be that jealous about what another person is doing. You feel secure enough in yourself, you're going to let somebody else be an autonomous, functioning individual, too. You are worried you are going to lose the person. Young people typically have a lot of insecurities about who they are and what they are worth. So it's normal for an adolescent to be insecure—and the jealousy comes from that insecurity. You need to move in the other direction, to start focusing on developing yourself and your productivity and doing things you value.

Q: What about if you're not the one who's doing the breaking up? What's the best way to deal with it—and the worst?

Dr. Drew: The worst way is to act out in a way that's irreversible: You hurt somebody, you hurt yourself. You lose a job. If you act out by increasing the loss in some way because of your anger or rage—that's the worst way.

Adam: You'll get over the event, the actual breakup, with the passing of time. Maybe a month. Maybe fifteen months—but you'll get past it. But if you do some permanent damage, well, permanent means forever.

If you kill someone and go to prison for twenty years—hey, you might have gotten over the relationship in twenty weeks. Or if you get drunk, go speeding into the night on your motorcycle, and wind up putting yourself in a wheelchair, well, you're over that girl pretty quick—but you're never going to walk again.

So here's the rule: Don't screw up anything that's going to last longer than the period of time it would take you to get over the person anyway. If you go out and shoot the chick's new boyfriend and go to prison for fifteen to twenty years, well, gee, you'll probably be over the relationship the first six months in the pen. And now you have to deal with the by-product of that, which is prison or the wheelchair or heroin addiction, whatever it is.

Q: What's the best way?

Adam: Try to save some dignity. You've already been robbed of some of it when you've been dumped. So try to cut your losses.

Dr. Drew: We talked about the depressions we both experienced in these kind of breakups. Those are really where you end up making bad choices and losing it—sort of going down a slippery slope as a result of the unpleasant feelings you may be carrying around every day and not know it.

Adam: You're begging the girl to get back together with you and it's one of these negative cycles where, once you get into it, you lose some dignity, you take a beating—and then you lose a little more during the process and that makes you more vulnerable to attempt it again. Eventually, you're to the point where you just don't care. You're so tortured and downtrodden, you're in such pain that you don't care—you just want to act out. You just need a release.

Dr. Drew: You need relief. But it becomes this desperate attempt to reconcile the relationship, which is pathetic. You desperately try to get back together and it becomes just a pathetic move.

Adam: I can remember making bets with myself not to call: I said, "I am not going to call this person for a week. I've called them five times in the last six days and it's pathetic. They haven't called me back."

Dr. Drew: But making deals with yourself is a bad sign.

Adam: A bad sign. "One week—no phone calls." I think I made it maybe a day.

Dr. Drew: It's like an addict saying, "I'm going to go a week without any heroin." Or an alcoholic making a deal with himself, saying, "I'll drink only on the weekends."

Adam: There's just no possible way. So try to have a little dignity. It hurts, but you'll feel better about yourself in the long run.

Celebrity Input ★ *from Comic Marlon Wayans*

★ ★ ★ ★ **Q: I broke up with this girl after six months and she won't stop calling me and getting into arguments with me. I'm really over her but can't get her out of my life. What do you suggest?**

★ **Marlon:** I suggest you stop sleeping with her. Maybe she'd stop calling you then. That's what guys do: "I can't understand why she keeps calling me." Well, maybe if you would stop putting your penis in her, that would maybe take away some of the attraction.

Adam: I always say if you really want to get rid of someone, you've got to treat them like a stray cat in your backyard. If you leave food out—even just a little bit of food out a couple times a week—the cat's going to hang out.

★ **Marlon:** Guys do that on purpose. Sometimes you have lonely days and that little stray pussy cat can really help you out. Then you want to put a little bit of Tender Vittles out there.

Adam: Right. But let's just say he's dead serious about getting rid of her for good. My take is this: If you don't give the person anything to go off of, even the craziest person is going to get bored and move on.

★ **Marlon:** Just change your number and let her down gently. If that doesn't work, then change the number and move to Africa and pretty soon she won't be bothering you.

Dr. Drew: What we normally do is tell people to cut off all communication. Most people who are in situations like this are busily trying to let the other person down softly, because they don't want to feel guilty about hurting the other person. But they hurt them even more as a result. So my advice is to cut off and end all communication. If you can't do it, if you work with the person or share a class at school, you have to find some way to create a boundary and just end the communication. Be-

ADAM on the Difference Between the Way Men and Women Take a Breakup

Here's an example of women being much more in tune with this stuff than guys:

I'd just been broken up with and was trying to shake myself out of this stupor. So I went out with a guy friend to some honky-tonk bar—just to do something other than sit around feeling sorry for myself.

We see a couple of girls, and even though they were pretty scary-looking we said, "Let's go talk to them. We just need to get the ball rolling here." So we go up to them—and these were, quite frankly, hideous, bad women.

I said, "Hello, ladies, do you mind if I sit down here?"

And one of them said, "Why?"

And I thought, *Jesus Christ, I'm getting shit kicked out of me by ugly women.* And I realized that it's got to be more than a coincidence. There wasn't anything physically wrong with me; I was in decent shape.

But I was just so wretched—and women can sense that, the way a wild animal senses fear in its prey.

I mean, there's nothing a guy would like more than to find a distraught woman who is looking to rebound from a bad breakup, who wants basically to drown her sorrows in alcohol and flop at the first empty apartment she can find. To a guy, this is great: When some good-looking chick is a mess because her boyfriend dumped her, we're going to pounce—like she's a pot roast and we're the hyena.

But women take one look at a guy in the same situation and say, "This guy is pathetic. Get lost." It's almost as if they've released some sort of composite on you through the female ranks that says, "Watch out for this guy—he's pathetic and horny."

cause even negative interaction is still a relationship; some people will cling to that as a faint hope that they can restore the relationship they dream of. If they have no contact with you, they'll begin to get over it and to focus on someone else.

12

Sexually Transmitted Diseases, or STDs

Q: I've got something on my penis, like a bubble. It hurts when I squeeze it and now it's turned into a sore. What is it?

Dr. Drew: Usually blisters that ulcerate are herpes. In any case, it needs to be seen by a doctor. Anything painful on the penis, on the genitalia, is sort of really considered herpes until proven otherwise. Usually other things that ulcerate, like syphilis or chancroid, tend not to be painful. Again, this is something that needs to be looked at by a doctor. Doctors are used to looking at various growths and things; it's nothing that you should be embarrassed about. It's what we're there for.

Q: How do you get a sexually transmitted disease?

Dr. Drew: It depends on the disease. If it's a blood-borne STD, it's usually the result of exposure to some body fluid where the infectious organism is present. These are usually viruses and so the virus gets into the other person's bloodstream and begins infecting that person.

Syphilis is usually transmitted at the site of the chancres or rash. Those points of contact tend to be highly concentrated in the spirochetes of the disease. It's the same thing with herpes, because the virus is excreted in the herpes lesions. Gonorrhea, chlamydia, nongonococcal urethritis—all are usually caused by contact with a mucous membrane, such as sexual intercourse, where the urethra and its contents are exposed to the vagina and the cervix. It can also be through oral-to-genital contact, because the mouth is an environment that can be infected through this sort of contact.

Q: Can you get an STD even if you've had unprotected sex only once?

Dr. Drew: Yes, with any of them, theoretically, and with many of them, almost certainly: herpes, venereal warts, syphilis, gonorrhea, chlamydia.

Q: How prevalent are sexually transmitted diseases?

Dr. Drew: They seem to be down a little bit, although there's a lot of anxiety about it. I think we've been successful in teaching young people about it.

Adam: I just heard a report that says younger men in the gay community are getting relaxed about safe sex because they keep hearing about a cure for AIDS being on the horizon. So condom use is down, that sort of thing.

Dr. Drew: Still, I think young people have changed their behavior. For instance, we hear people talking about having tons of partners and what they're talking about is five. So there seems to be a lot less sexual acting out; at least in some socioeconomic brackets, STD rates are going down. There is a lot of panic about warts—but everything is AIDS in most people's minds when you mention STDs.

Q: What are the most common STDs today?

Dr. Drew: Most studies suggest that about 30 percent of the sexually active population has venereal warts. Herpes is somewhere between 5 and 30 percent, depending on what data you read—

Adam: Warts is 30 percent?

Dr. Drew: They're very common. It depends on what data you look at. If you look at it nationally, it is very common. The number is very high.

Adam: I have an idea. A lot of people aren't particularly sophisticated. They're trying to figure out whether their partner is packing something, whether it's warts or herpes or whatever. They can't really tell. Women have a lot of stuff they may not be aware of. You hear these stories: Her gynecologist missed something and she ended up having to have a hysterectomy.

Now stay with me: They've got these drug-sniffing dogs—and this is not an exaggeration—that can sniff out a joint packed in coffee grounds welded into a car bumper. They can train these dogs to sniff out fruit for the Department of Agriculture, or kielbasa or coke or heroin in suitcases.

So here's my idea: We should have venereal-sniffing dogs, venereal dogs, VDs for short. They can sniff out crabs or herpes or whatever. Just hop right up there on the gynecological examining table, working for the doctor. Hey, dogs put their noses in your crotch anyway. Just a quick pass, a little sniff, sniff, and then it stops and barks. I bet we could train a dog—don't tell me we couldn't train a dog to sniff for crabs, or at least a yeast infection. They can find marijuana packed in coffee grounds—don't tell me they couldn't find something through a skirt and panties.

MYTHBUSTERS

Myth: *Venereal warts are painful.*

The truth, according to Dr. Drew:

Warts are warts. If you have ever had a wart on your hand or your knee or your arm, that's a wart. It feels the same when they occur on genitalia. They do not hurt; they usually go unnoticed, and in men they have no consequence. In women, they can increase the risk of cervical cancer. That risk can be eliminated by more aggressive screening, through more frequent Pap smears and treatment. Sometimes, they also can be detected by an added exam called a colposcopy, which is basically looking at the cervix under a microscope. Most wart viruses tend to eventually go away with time or treatment.

MYTHBUSTERS

Myth: *Herpes can't be transmitted if I'm not having an outbreak.*

The truth, according to Dr. Drew: The herpesvirus can be shed at any time, even when there is no outbreak. However, the concentration of virus is much higher and the likelihood of transmission is substantially greater when someone is having an outbreak.

Q: What are the rules of STD etiquette? When do you tell someone you have it—and how do you do it?

Adam: Drew will always say, "Well, you sit down and you tell the person quite honestly that you have the herpesvirus and that you'll be wearing a condom during the lovemaking." And I always think, oh, boy, what world does that conversation occur in?

Dr. Drew: But what if the person actually had a relationship first, they were dating awhile and then something developed?

Adam: I had sex with someone who had herpes and she told me afterward.

Dr. Drew: How did that go?

Adam: I was so delighted and thankful she had sex with me that I didn't press the issue.

Dr. Drew: How did she happen to tell you afterward?

Adam: I wore a condom, so I think that was her rationale for not having said anything. Afterward, she said, "Oh, it was good you did that."

Dr. Drew: But how did it come up afterward? Why did she let it go at all?

Adam: Because the relationship was starting to form a little bit and I think she felt compelled to say something.

Dr. Drew: And you ended the relationship right there?

Adam: No. I was thankful she was willing to have me. Two weeks later, she ended it. Bad deal.

I have a friend who has herpes and he tells me, "I wear a condom every time and I tell them every time." And he doesn't seem to have a problem with it. And in a way, maybe this approach could work to your advantage.

Say you're in a developing relationship—you haven't had sex yet but you've had a few dates and things are looking like they might go in that direction. So you say, "Listen, I really enjoy you and I'm attracted to you. I'd like to be intimate with you. And because I respect you, I want to tell you I have the herpesvirus. I'll wear a condom and there shouldn't be any difficulty." Now she almost has to have sex with you. Because if she doesn't, it's only because of the virus. It's like minority hiring or something. There's a certain retarded, backward logic that could be effective here.

Celebrity Input

★ from Comic Marlon Wayans

★ ★ ★ **Q: I had oral sex with a girl who was having her period. Can I catch a disease that way?**

Dr. Drew: There is probably a slightly increased risk of blood-borne disorders like HIV and hepatitis. Those are things you should worry about. In fact, it's not, shall we say, the giving partner who is in most significant jeopardy. During their periods, in and around their periods, women are at higher risk of ascending infection: infections of the uterus and fallopian tubes. If there is anything in your mouth, it is more likely to cause serious consequences with her.

★ **Marlon:** I do think there is some kind of law that you go directly to hell. I mean, I'm pretty sure she's happy, but if I was your mom getting a hello kiss in the morning, I would be pretty upset with you.

Adam: Oh, that is just foul.

★ **Marlon:** I would never let that guy sip out of my soda. Let's put it that way.

Adam: I tell you, my hat's off to the guy. I mean—that's love.

★ **Marlon:** He's a better man than me.

Adam: That's an A for effort right there.

MYTHBUSTERS

Myth: *Having anal sex is a way of preventing STDs.*

The truth, according to Dr. Drew: STDs are generally transmitted via mucous membranes: the lining of the mouth, the lining of the rectum, the lining of the vagina. It's a layer that is thinner than skin but still separates the body from the outside world. Whenever a virus or bacterium comes in contact with one of these mucous membranes, it can enter the bloodstream and the body. Typically the viral STDs such as AIDS or hepatitis C actually require some body fluid to be passed. The rectal membrane is particularly susceptible to this kind of transmission during anal sex.

Q: What are the consequences of leaving an STD untreated?

Dr. Drew: A very common consequence is infertility, especially in women. The most common cause of infertility in this country is *Chlamydia,* a bacterial organism. Women can get abscesses in the pelvis, as well as more generalized infections called pelvic inflammatory disease. Venereal warts can proliferate if left untreated, and ultimately some of the wart viruses are associated with cervical cancer. It's a little-publicized fact that venereal warts are associated with risk of anal cancer when they occur there.

For men, there could be infertility as well. STDs can also cause chronic prostate infections, pain, swelling testicles, infection, and inflammation within the testicles. Gonorrhea can even cause a serious form of arthritis.

Reported Cases of Sexually Transmitted Diseases in the U.S., 1996

Syphilis	Gonorrhea	Chlamydia
Men: 27,030	Men: 164,871	Men: 74,336
Women: 25,916	Women: 160,647	Women: 414,528

(*Source: Centers for Disease Control and Prevention*)

DR. DREW explains STDs, Their Symptoms and Treatments

- **Syphilis:** This is an infectious disease that has affected mankind for centuries. Until the nineteenth century, it was the equivalent of HIV: a potentially devastating disease that had no cure. It wasn't until the twentieth century and the discovery of penicillin and other antibiotics that it could be treated and cured. It still remains a common and highly contagious disease spread by sexual contact, whose initial symptom is a chancre or ulcer at the point of contact, typically on the mouth or genitals. The chancre will disappear after a few weeks; when the disease moves into the secondary stage, its symptom is a rash, which is quite infectious. If left untreated, it can develop into a variety of medical problems and ultimately to final stage, or tertiary syphilis, which can cause dementia.
- **Gonorrhea:** This disease is spread by sexual contact. In men, the symptoms are painful urination and a thick whitish discharge from the tip of the penis. In women, symptoms include vaginal discharge, vaginal irritation, painful urination, and pelvic pain. Gonorrhea can cause pelvic inflammatory disease, abscesses, and arthritis. It is usually treated with antibiotics.
- **Chlamydia:** This is a bacterial type of organism that in women can cause a very low-grade infection that gets into the fallopian tubes and stays there for long periods of time, potentially without women knowing about it. It destroys the small hair cells within the tubes that move the egg from the ovary to the uterus. It scars the tubes so they don't work properly and the egg can never get to the uterus so there cannot be implantation. In men, it can cause prostate and testicular infections. It is treated with antibiotics. The initial symptoms may be indistinguishable from gonorrhea.
- **Herpes:** This is a sexually transmitted virus that is very common and is part of the same family of viruses as cold sores or canker sores. Once you have it,

you've got it forever. Any painful outbreak in the genital region should be considered herpes unless proven otherwise. In men, it usually takes the form of clustered blisters on the penis that burn and hurt. In women, the blisters may go unnoticed because they are internal—on the cervix or inside the vagina. These can cause discomfort and burning, but women sometimes mistake this for a yeast infection. The initial outbreak is often the worst and may last a week or two. Once it heals, it will recur at intervals that vary from person to person. Once you have herpes, you are potentially contagious forever—but more contagious when you have an outbreak or rash of blisters. Herpes can lead to cervical cancer in women; aside from the discomfort of outbreaks, there are no documented long-term effects in men. While there are no drugs to cure the disease, there are antiviral drugs that can help shorten the duration of each outbreak and increase the interval between outbreaks.

- **Genital warts:** These are just what the name says: warts that occur on the genitals. They are caused by a virus and are passed through sexual contact. Like herpes, once you've got it, you could always be potentially contagious, even when the warts are not present. Though the virus tends to wane with time, it also tends to multiply and spread and is harder to control in women because it occurs inside the vagina, as well as outside. Warts can be associated with cervical cancer in women and anal cancer in both genders. They can be treated by burning them off with a cauterizing tool, laser, or liquid nitrogen, or by using a substance called interferon (which is injected) or podophyllin, a liquid that's applied to the warts. There also is a new cream that has just been released that seems to be very effective for external warts.
- **Hepatitis:** There are two strains of hepatitis that can be transmitted sexually. Hepatitis B is very contagious and is common among homosexuals. It can cause a destructive infection of the liver and can lead to cirrhosis and liver failure. It can be prevented with a vaccine; children routinely are being vaccinated and IV drug users, homosexuals, and health-care workers should

be vaccinated. Hepatitis C is less contagious and is transmitted in ways similar to HIV: through the exchange of bodily fluids. While it causes a milder form of hepatitis, it, too, leads to chronic liver disease and liver cancer. While there are treatments for chronic forms of hepatitis C, there is no cure, and as yet no vaccine.

13

HIV and AIDS

Q: What is HIV?

Dr. Drew: HIV stands for human immune-deficiency virus. It is a retrovirus, a package of ribonucleic acids packed in a protein shell that has the capacity to bind with certain human cells and invade those cells. It uses the cells to replicate itself, then goes out and infects other cells. It tends to attack a certain limb of the white blood cell systems that paralyzes some part of the immune system.

Q: How do you get HIV?

Dr. Drew: For people who already are infected, it's present in most body fluids, although in very low concentrations initially. As the virus is allowed to replicate unchecked, there is a higher concentration as AIDS develops and people become more infected. If you're exposed to someone else's blood or vascular system, it's an opportunity for the virus to get into your bloodstream and begin infecting you. It happens with any exchange of body fluid across a mucosal surface, such as the vagina, rectum, mouth, nose, eyes, urethra. You're also at risk if you have an open wound and it is exposed to body fluids of someone who is infected. This can also be through the shared use of hypodermic needles between people who are infected and those who aren't.

Q: What's the difference between HIV and AIDS?

Dr. Drew: AIDS is acquired immune-deficiency syndrome. It's a disease caused by HIV, and characteristically is the effect of the destruction of the body's immune function. HIV makes the body vulnerable to AIDS-related infections that normally wouldn't be able to thrive or to tumors that would not otherwise develop. AIDS is a formal diagnosis of infection by one of a number of opportunistic infections as well as unusual tumors, wasting, and dementia.

Q: Who is most at risk from AIDS and HIV?

Dr. Drew: The largest increase in risk is among heterosexual teens, largely as a result of contact with IV drug users. Also, IV drug users, particularly heroin users, because heroin use is on the rise. AIDS is the most common killer of young males, greater than accidents—and it's becoming a common killer of heterosexual teens.

Q: Is AIDS something everyone should be afraid of?

Dr. Drew: It's been kind of overstated in this country. The risk of HIV is real; on the other hand, if you're not participating in these risky behaviors, the danger is minimal. To a certain extent, that danger has been exaggerated to get people to change their behavior—and it's worked. It took a long time, like a whole generation. At first they absorbed the information but it didn't change their behavior. By the next generation, this Y generation that's coming along, has begun to get it.

You can't really say the way it is presented to the public is wrong or inaccurate. It was just dramatized a little bit because that's the way we've always had to do things with humans. You have to create these huge barriers to contain their behavior.

Celebrity Input

★ from Actor French Stewart

★ ★ ★ **Q: My friends and I are into drinking blood as part of a sadomasochism thing we're into. Is there a risk to drinking blood?**

Adam: Is there risk? Well, there's always the chance someone might put a stake through your heart while you are sleeping.

★ **French:** I would say that, health risks aside: Get off the Depeche Mode record and cheer up. If you are a blood drinker, that's a crappy hobby.

Adam: Hey, referees and trainers in the NBA wear surgical gloves in case some guy gets an elbow to the cheek, on the off chance that they might get a spatter of blood on them. Imagine how much you're ingesting and where it's coming from.

I'm not a doctor but I work with one and I can tell you that this is what's known as high-risk behavior. It seems like a hobby that'd be hard to keep up with.

Dr. Drew: This is the kind of blood exposure that you worry about in terms of contracting the blood-borne sexually transmitted diseases like hepatitis C, HIV, hepatitis B, and God knows what other blood-borne conditions. You don't know where the blood is coming from or what that person has been exposed to. You're used to thinking in terms of sexually transmitted diseases, but there are plenty of other blood-borne disorders that you could potentially be exposed to that way.

★ **French:** Absolutely. It's not like you trade baseball cards, for God's sake. I suppose that there's something romantic tied in with the whole vampire thing, especially if you are fifteen and your little chemicals are going crazy and you are depressed and your emotions are ripping out of your body like crazy. All I can say is, I can't imagine any good will come from this.

Q: Why should you always take precautions against AIDS with a new sex partner?

Dr. Drew: For the same reason you shouldn't fly in an airplane without putting your seat belt on. The chances the plane is going to crash are pretty slim but—

Adam: Hold on, that's a horrible analogy. Drew, don't do analogies. What we're talking about is getting in the car and not putting on a seat belt, or getting on a motorcycle without a helmet. There's a real slim chance that you're going to get in an accident when you get in your car or on your motorcycle—but if you do, you could die.

Dr. Drew: The data on seat belts are pretty interesting. If you don't wear the seat belt 100 percent of the time, your benefits drop off dramatically. If you start taking your seat belt off for local driving, your risk of serious harm shoots up.

Adam: If you don't wear your seat belt 10 percent of the time, it doesn't make you safe 90 percent of the time.

Dr. Drew: Exactly.

Adam: So the argument is a fairly obvious one: HIV is so permanent and so potentially deadly that that's what makes it not worth the risk. Think of it like gambling, and you're spinning the big wheel. You have almost no chance that it's going to land on double zero. But the bet is, if it lands on double zero, they get to take your house and your car and clean you out. It makes sense to put down a little insurance; maybe it costs you five bucks and it's never going to land there—but if it does, you're screwed unless you buy the insurance. If it landed on double zero and cost you only five hundred dollars, you'd just spin it because even if it lands there, it's not going to break you. That's like getting crabs—landing on double zero and having to pay five hundred dollars. But the other way—where you can potentially lose everything—you just don't want to take that chance.

Q: Is a condom alone enough to protect you from HIV during sex?

Dr. Drew: It's a start. The most important thing is not putting yourself at risk.

Adam: Let's say you do, though. Is the condom the only thing you can use?

Dr. Drew: You should also be using dental dams against potential oral transmissions.

Adam: Are there any other barriers besides the dental dam and the condom?

Dr. Drew: No.

Adam: So that's it.

Dr. Drew: You otherwise have to try to avoid body fluids.

Adam: Isn't that kind of bizarre? That, after all these years and all these people, there's only one form of barrier for HIV and AIDS and that's the condom?

Here's what we need to do: The women need some sort of fogger they could put down there like what you do when your house has fleas. You clear out for a day, pull the pin—it kills everything in the area. Or a woman needs some sort of tablet or something that just holes up in there, and basically anything that's living there is dead or rendered useless for three or four hours. Can't they have something like that? With the penis, we need a dip of some sort. I think that would do it.

Dr. Drew: I don't think people use latex barriers in enough situations. They certainly don't pay attention to deep kissing and oral sex. And oral sex definitely is a potential route. Virtually any STD that can be transmitted genitally can be transmitted orally, back and forth in either direction.

Q: At what point should you get an HIV test?

Dr. Drew: It's already part of a routine health screening. Insurance companies screen for it for any kind of insurance you want to get. Whenever I admit an IV drug user to my drug unit, I test them. The same thing with someone who's had sex with a heroin addict.

I think it's good that people who are going to be engaged in sexual activity know what each other's status is. You simply say, "Have you been tested?" That's simple enough. I think young people are finally coming around to that as part of normal sexual etiquette, along with having and using condoms. Because you can never be 100 percent sure. All you can do is protect yourself. The most sensible thing is not to put yourself in harm's way. It is the healthy and responsible thing to do.

Adam: I wouldn't be messing with needles—or messing with people with needles. Or people who have been involved with dangerous behavior.

Dr. Drew: But if you find you have been with a partner who has been involved in risky behavior before having sex with you—then you should see your doctor and have yourself tested. If someone has had more than ten partners, if they've engaged in homosexual experimentation of any kind, if they have a history of IV drug usage—those are high-risk behaviors.

As soon as you think you've been put at risk, get the test. Then get it again six months later. It takes about six months for the immune system to react to the virus, creating the antibodies that are commonly measured in the blood.

DR. DREW on HIV Testing and AIDS Symptoms

If you believe you've been exposed to HIV, you can now just go to your pharmacy and buy a very effective home-HIV test that involves scraping some cells from the inside of your cheek and sending it in to a test center to receive a result. And the accuracy level is very high.

What the test doesn't provide, however, is counseling for people when they get the results. And I believe there should be counseling, no matter what the result.

If the result is positive, you need counseling on what your next steps should be, in terms of how to find the kind of medications you need to keep the HIV virus from turning into full-blown AIDS. It has recently been shown that, after a definite exposure, infection with HIV may be preventable with certain antiviral drugs. If you believe you've been exposed, you should get on antiviral drugs, because they can prevent the infection from taking hold—and can prevent the progression from HIV to AIDS. You also need someone to talk to, to help you handle the psychological fallout of such potentially heavy news. You also need to be reminded of your responsibilities toward others, to help you keep from spreading the virus to others—as well as figuring out how to tell those you may already have exposed.

Even if your test comes back negative, you need to talk to a counselor for some of the same reasons. If you took a test, it probably was because you were afraid you had been exposed; a counselor can give you much-needed advice on how to avoid exposure in the future. A counselor may also be able to assess whether you should test yourself again in the future and how often.

In either case, I suggest you seek help at an alternative test site or an organization that is used to providing care to HIV-positive individuals. These kinds of clinics and centers will provide straight, nonjudgmental information that could save your life.

HIV itself typically has no symptoms, though 98+ percent of those people who have contracted the virus will test positive within six months of exposure. There is also a test that can show how much of the virus is in the blood: the viral-load test for the antibody. The more there is, the more your immune system is being compromised and the more likely you are to show symptoms of AIDS-related illnesses. This test is now being used to monitor the effectiveness of antiviral drugs in suppressing the production of virus and thereby delaying the disease's progress.

With an acute HIV infection, the first symptoms are similar to mononucleosis or the flu: high fever, sore throat, swollen glands. These last anywhere from three to ten days; they can be mild enough to pass off as flu or severe enough to put you in the hospital. It's at this point that HIV antibodies usually can be detected.

Once HIV turns into AIDS, the symptoms become more severe. Among the more common signs are night sweats, fatigue, unexplained weight loss, the appearance of lesions (Kaposi's sarcoma), diarrhea, recurrent cough or pneumonia, even dementia. Theoretically, however, catching HIV before it has a chance to compromise the immune system gives you a better chance to change your health habits and to use some of the many new drugs that seem to be effective at minimizing the amount of virus in your system, or even stopping the virus in its tracks and preventing it from becoming AIDS.

14

Homosexuality

MYTHBUSTERS

Myth: *Men who dream about having sex with other men are actually latent homosexuals who are hiding their true natures.*

The truth, according to Dr. Drew: Nothing of the sort. Our selection of sexual orientation is a complex phenomenon. All of us have some sexual feelings toward the same sex. Things that might be otherwise overwhelming or uncomfortable to us often come out in dreams. Same-sex dreams are very common, particularly in middle and late adolescence. You are more likely to have a same-sex dream than you would be to admit to feelings of same-sex attraction.

Q: I've always assumed I'm a straight woman. But I find someone of the same sex sexually attractive. What does that mean?

Dr. Drew: It means you're in the presence of Cindy Crawford.

Adam: I think everyone can dabble in that.

Dr. Drew: It's whether there is intent along with attraction. To be aroused by the same sex—that happens to everybody at some time in their lives.

Adam: Right—there has to be a certain malice in your penis. For women, it's much more common and natural.

Q: What should I do if I think I might be gay?

Dr. Drew: This is a common thing. We encourage young people who have same-sex feelings to not feel threatened or alarmed by them and to understand that pretty much everybody at some time in their development will have same-sex attractions. Women particularly will confuse warm, intimate feelings with physical attraction.

We generally tell people not to act out on those feelings of confusion. Just because they have the same-sex attraction doesn't mean they're bisexual; it doesn't mean they're gay. It may mean they're going through usual development. This may be the awakening of homosexuality or they may just be confused and ambivalent. If they still have ambivalence about their sexual orientation at nineteen or twenty—and, oh, by the way, they tell us they had a terrible trauma that contributed to that—that's confusion about sexual orientation and identity.

Q: Why shouldn't I act on those feelings when they first present themselves?

Dr. Drew: Because the average person having those feelings at fifteen or sixteen, if he or she has sex, is going to worsen his or her confusion.

Let's say a clearly homosexual or heterosexual person chooses to have sex at fifteen or sixteen: That in itself is going to be traumatic for them because they're not quite developed to be able to handle it, even with a clear-cut sense of themselves and their sexuality.

Even people who are clear about their sexuality can be adversely affected by getting involved physically at a young age. Now, if they're acting out when they're confused, that will only contribute to difficulty and confusion in development.

We don't discourage a twenty-year-old from experimenting. Maybe you are gay. If you're really having strong feelings for guys, women, whoever, so be it. Maybe this is part of a burgeoning homosexual orientation; maybe you're bisexual. By that age, one should have a much clearer sense of one's identity, sexual or otherwise.

But if it's someone who's twenty and they were sexually abused at five and have talked to us about their confusion, we're going to say, "Look, there's going to be a lot of chaos in your relationships. Be careful. Try to stay with one person. Get some therapy and see if that confusion doesn't sort itself out."

Adam: We don't talk to that many homosexuals who haven't had some form of abuse in their lives. Now you've got to realize that they're talking to us because they have a problem; they're not happy that they're gay. So this isn't all gay people we're talking about.

I really used to be under the impression that you were either gay or you weren't and that was about it. What the hell could you do? It's the way you were born and I didn't think much about it. But I realize now that a fairly large percentage—or a much higher percentage than people either know or will admit—a large percentage of bisexuals, gays, and lesbians have had less-than-satisfactory childhoods and that has been a factor in determining their sexuality. But it's not politically correct to say, "The reason you're gay is because you were molested."

Dr. Drew: Again, this is based on the people we speak to.

★ *from Actress Janeane Garofalo*

★ ★ ★ **Q: I've always dated women, and want to get married one day and have kids. But recently I've met a guy while I was on a business trip. We kind of hit it off and I guess we wound up being intimate. Am I gay?**

Dr. Drew: I have heard this story from many gay men, both in clinical settings and casually, that particularly these young males or young adults didn't want to be gay. Not that they didn't acknowledge their gay feelings. But they just wanted so badly to fulfill the image of the adult they expected to grow up to be.

MYTHBUSTERS

Myth: *You're born gay. Or: Being gay is a matter of choice.*

The truth, according to Dr. Drew: Both these positions oversimplify a very complex issue. Homosexuality appears to be a product of both nature and nurture. That is to say there is probably some element of genetic predisposition in a given individual. But environment and development also play a part. People don't make a choice to be homosexual. In fact, many homosexual male teens often will go through many months or years of denying their homosexual feelings, trying to live a heterosexual lifestyle; they often would give anything not to be gay. At that age, it can be terribly painful to confront one's homosexuality. By doing so, a young person opens himself up to ridicule from his peers. It's also very painful to give up one's image of how one is likely to be in the future. I had one friend say that admitting he was gay was like killing his parents.

And that included wife and kids; many of them go so far as getting married and having kids.

Adam: I wouldn't intellectualize the decision too much. If you label yourself, then you sort of have to commit to one lifestyle or the next, and then you may go against whatever your impulse is. But I wouldn't try to map it out now. And yes, I think if you gave a guy a blow job on a business trip, you are gay.

But I don't understand that. I mean, if that isn't what your proclivity is, why would you do it? I'll hear guys say, "Yeah, I slipped up, I had a beer, I was at a party, one thing led to another." To me that just means you are in denial. What I'm saying is: You are either in or you are out. You go on a business trip, you go away for a couple of days, you give a guy a reach-around—you are in. Which is fine. Just go ahead and say, "That's what I do." No problem.

★ **Janeane:** There are so many married gay people that we see. And a lot of them are very famous because there are many famous people who can't possibly admit that they are gay, and they have wives and children.

Dr. Drew: Why is that?

★ **Janeane:** Fear.

Dr. Drew: Fear of rejection if they show their real selves?

★ **Janeane:** I don't know if there are still so many people in 1998 who can't bear the thought of being gay. But I think it goes back to bad parenting. Some people are scared of their parents.

Dr. Drew: I think this guy is probably gay, and that he isn't really accepting that yet. I would look very carefully at what his sexual orientation is before I did something like get married.

Q: Are people gay because of the environment they come from? Or is it because they're born that way?

Dr. Drew: There's an argument that it's a biological predisposition, that there's a different genetic or brain structure between gay and nongay people. They're not arguing that there's no environmental influence, but they're saying that the biology may have more to do with it than we otherwise think. That you have to be predisposed. That for some people who are biologically predisposed, environmental influence may be very slight and needn't be much at all. In fact, this pretty much describes most controversies as they pertain to human behavior: nature vs. nurture.

Adam: Well, ultimately, I don't care. I wish a higher percentage of the community was homosexual. In general, I think they're better participants in the community and in the world at large. I think there's a higher percentage of homosexuals who recycle. They take better care of themselves. They're less violent. They manage their finances better. Plus they're not having a bunch of screwed-up kids who we have to pay for.

Here's my take on all colors and proclivities: As long as I'm not banging you, I don't care what you do. Then the emphasis shifts to what are you doing for the community or to hurt the community. That's when I start judging. And, as far as gays and lesbians go, God bless them. They're not overpopulating, they're not overpolluting. They're working at their jobs and taking care of their skin.

Q: Are you either gay or straight? Or are there true bisexuals?

Adam: If you're a guy, you're either gay or you're straight.

Dr. Drew: I think there is such a thing, but it's much easier for a woman to be bisexual for a number of reasons, both sociological and psychological. There is such a thing as a mature bisexual orientation, but it's relatively uncommon. The most common thing we see is the homosexual male who doesn't want to accept his sexual orientation. So he keeps trying to have a heterosexual life. Or it's someone who has a good deal of ambivalence about his sexuality, usually from some sort of sexual or physical abuse from his childhood.

Q: When should you come out?

Adam: After your folks die.

Dr. Drew: You should be coming out when you're clear in your orientation. When you're planning to commit to that lifestyle. Probably when you have a stable relationship, when you have a sufficient network of supportive peers of a similar persuasion to fall back upon, to relate to, to give you support when you stand up and get counted.

Because there will be a reaction. You will have people hurting you. And if you don't have the right support there, it could be devastating.

Q: Why should you come out?

Dr. Drew: It's not always necessary. But I can understand that people would want important people in their lives to relate to them and to who they actually are. The more you hide from and lie to a person, the more hollow your relationships are. The beauty and the treachery of primary relationships is they tend to be templates for other relationships you carry out, too. So it is an important breeding ground for healthy relationships. It's important for these to be honest and open.

Adam: Here's the deal. I don't believe people at work need to know. I don't believe that anybody who could possibly use it in a harmful way against you needs to know anything—any more than a criminal needs to know your PIN number at the ATM.

MYTHBUSTERS

Myth: *A transvestite is the same as a transsexual—and both are homosexual.*

The truth, according to Dr. Drew: A transvestite is a male who enjoys dressing like a female, but he's not necessarily gay. Typically, it's someone with some sort of fetish or preoccupation with taking on a female persona. It is a way of defending against and dealing with more threatening feelings that remain on the subconscious level, and he often needs this behavior to function sexually.

A transsexual is an individual who wishes to switch genders—to have an operation that would change their sexual organs from either male to female or vice versa. Oddly enough, many of the male-to-female transsexuals I have cared for over the years wind up in lesbian relationships with women. While it seems confusing, it apparently is not at all uncommon.

THE GAY APTITUDE TEST

Give yourself points according to the scale below:

- If you know the difference between eyeliner and mascara: +2 **points.**
- For every Broadway show tune you know the words to: +3 **points.**
- For each of those that is by Stephen Sondheim: +10 **points.**
- If you've ever pronounced the word *vase* as *vahz*: +5 **points.**
- If you know the difference between taupe and mauve: +5 **points.**
- If you can pronounce taupe and mauve: +10 **points.**
- An Erasure concert ticket stub on your dresser: +15 **points.**
- If you know what a tea cozy is: +3 **points.**
- For each cardigan sweater in your closet: +5 **points.**
- For each argyle sweater vest: +10 **points.**
- If you've ever gotten a professional massage that didn't involve an Asian woman and a handjob: +10 **points.**
- If you've ever taken a "me" day: +15 **points.**
- If you've ever paid more than $8 for a haircut: +5 **points.**
- For each scented candle you own: +5 **points.**
- For each scented candle that smells like a guy's ass: +20 **points.**
- If you own a mustache comb: +5 **points.**
- If you've ever sweated, or even lightly perspired, to "The Oldies": +10 **points.**
- For every pair of shoes you own with a buckle: +2 **points.**
- For every pair of shoes you own with tassels: +3 **points.**
- If you've named your penis: –5 **points.**
- If you've named your roommate's penis: +15 **points.**
- If you purchase underpants in quantities smaller than the Big Value 14-pair Chubpack: +5 **points**.
- If you purchase underpants with buckles or tassels: +10 **points.**

- If you're into aromatherapy: **+5 points.**
- If you think aromatherapy means farting in a sleeping bag: **−10 points.**

Scoring:

0–20: Gun buddies with Charlton Heston.
21–40: Ready to cruise Hollywood Boulevard with Hugh Grant.
41–60: Ready to cruise Hollywood Boulevard with Eddie Murphy.
61–80: Regular patron of Liberace Museum in Las Vegas.
81–100: You make Harvey Fierstein look butch.

Dr. Drew: It's the same as the fact that no one needs to know your private sexual preferences in bed. As long as it doesn't hurt anyone, it's nobody else's business.

Adam: A lot of gay men are fairly overt in their physicality anyway. They're crossing the street in front of you, and even when it's dark you're saying, "Okay, this guy's gay." It's a form of coming out to the world, when they swish down the street. I'm not quite sure what's behind that. I think I don't trust them any more than I trust the heterosexual man who's got the big Italian horn medallion and wears tank tops to weddings and funerals.

Anyone who needs to project not only their sexuality but anything—to me, they're on my list of people to avoid. Projecting that you're a tough guy—bad. Projecting that you're into the Gothic scene—bad. Projecting how much you're into this band or that music—bad. Projecting that you're heterosexual in a way-over-the-top way—it's all bad. I don't trust anybody who has to project that much about themselves.

So the gay men who I'm aware are gay by the way they talk or walk—that's projection. And I'm usually less likely to want to hang out with them. Now—what was the question?

Why should you come out? The only reason you come out is for yourself. I think I would come out only to people that it mattered to and not to everybody. Because I don't know what good is going to come from it—but there could be some potential harm. So why bother?

HOW TO HELP A FRIEND... *who has just come out as a gay person*

Dr. Drew: I would get them involved with other people who have been through that transition, possibly through gay and lesbian help centers. Encourage them to get professional help if they're severely depressed as a result of it or suicidal in any way.

Adam: Yeah, but it's pretty much just about finding a support network.

Dr. Drew: You should also acknowledge to that person that you still care about them, regardless of their sexual orientation. Be sure they know that you still love them, that you're still their friend. Just be available to them; don't get mad if they try to push you away and tell you that because you're not gay you can't understand what they're going through. It's their way of trying to manage their difficult feelings.

Q: How do you come out to your parents and your friends?

Adam: I'll tell you my plan on this. I don't think you do it with your partner present. I've said this many times and I believe it to be true: It's a volley directly into your parents' court. Parents already aren't good with you being gay. No matter what. Even the most liberal parents who love their children to death are at least mildly disappointed that their son is gay.

For men, the thought that your young son just blew a guy ten minutes ago—even for open-minded dads, it's not the most pleasant thought. So when you have the penis that you're blowing present while you're explaining that you enjoy blowing guys—it's just not the greatest feeling for parents.

It's sort of the equivalent of when a woman breaks up with you. If she says, "I'm breaking up with you because I want to go my way and sort my thing out and that's my scene," okay, fine, you can handle that. But if she says, "I'm with another guy and we've been together already and this is why we're breaking up—and oh, by the way, here he is"—that makes it that much tougher.

Dr. Drew: How would you do it? Write a letter? Call them on the phone?

Adam: Well, if I knew they were volatile, violent people—put it this way, I would not tell anyone who I didn't think was capable of handling it. Because they're almost asking not to be told. On a subconscious level, they're almost saying, "Don't tell me anything." What they're saying is, "I don't want to hear because I might spin out." And you know people who are that way.

So what do you do? You don't tell them anything. Don't say a word. If you have that type of person for a parent, I don't think you ever tell them. I really wouldn't. They could never get over it—and they could never handle it.

Dr. Drew: But if you have that kind of parents, you're probably pretty pissed off already. Telling them is one way of asserting yourself.

Adam: Parents like that are the ones people tend to want to tell. I say, don't do it.

But if you are going to tell them, I think I would tell them in person, like any news. Not at a holiday. Pick the parent who is more likely to be receptive and tell that parent first.

Dr. Drew: Whatever other support is available—sister, brother, cousin, whatever—get them involved.

Adam: And then, as cowardly as it may seem, tell them you're not currently seeing anybody.

Dr. Drew: "And I have to get back to school now." Do it as you're leaving to go to college.

Q: How should I deal with homophobia?

Adam: That's got to be rough, and here's why: People are racist, but they know enough to shut up about it whenever ethnicity comes near them. The people

The Lesbian Aptitude Test

Give yourself points according to the scale below:

- If you drive an El Camino: **+3 points.**
- If it has a lumbar rack: **+10 points.**
- For each pair of Birkenstocks in your closet: **+10 points.**
- For each pair of steel-toed boots: **+15 points.**
- If you've ever uttered the phrase "My friends call me Dutch": **+15 points.**
- For each dog you own: **+5 points.**
- If you breed Dobermans, mastiffs, or Rottweilers: **+15 points.**
- If you own a tennis racket autographed by Martina Navratilova: **+10 points.**
- If you ever quit your job to join the pro bowling tour: **+10 points.**
- If you own a Snap-On Tools catalog: **+5 points.**
- If you need to replace it more than twice a year: **+10 points.**
- If you need to replace it monthly: **+15 points.**
- If you refer to pants as dungarees: **+5 points.**
- If the knees of your dungarees are reinforced: **+15 points.**
- If you sport either of these hairdos: a fade or a mullet: **+10 points.**
- If your friends call you Mr. Goodwrench: **+10 points.**
- If you roll your own cigarettes: **+10 points.**
- If you can do it with one hand on your Harley's handlebars on the freeway: **+25 points.**
- If you've ever done any stage-diving: **+5 points.**
- If you did your stage-diving at Lilith Fair: **+10 points.**

Scoring:
0–20: Singing in the choir with Amy Grant and Marie Osmond.
21–40: Woodworking with Martha Stewart.
41–60: Starting to make Roseanne look feminine.
61–80: Lobbying with Chastity Bono.
81–100: Ellen DeGeneres considers you radical.

they're racist against are easy to pick out. But imagine you're some young guy, you're seventeen and gay but you're not out. And you're hanging around with your friends, guys you grew up with in the neighborhood, and that talk starts: "Hey, you're a homo. You faggot! You queer!" Not directed at him, but at each other, the way guys do. What the hell do you do with that?

Dr. Drew: The highest rate of completed suicide is the young homosexual male, and it's because of these issues. One is that, as we've discussed, they may have significant problems in their past—abuse, for the most part. But the more important thing is that they're so brutalized by their peers and sometimes even their family. They have nowhere to go and they don't know how to utilize support. They don't know other gay people because they're all not talking about it. They don't go to gay and lesbian youth centers and they are alone—very alone, because the families are equally unsupportive. And they don't have relationships yet, so it's horrible for them.

It's a time in their development when their single focus is on how they are accepted and perceived by their peers. They end up hating themselves.

Adam: Hey, if you get a zit, you don't go to school that day, you know? You feel too bad about yourself. Now imagine being gay and being tortured about that.

Q: So what should I do?

Dr. Drew: Well, as I said, there are gay and lesbian youth centers. If you're not comfortable going there, those places have help lines you can call. Basically, you need to find a support system, something that shows you that you're not that different, that it's okay to be gay and here's how you deal with it.

When to Tell Your Parents—and When Not To

Dr. Drew: I know there are many people who are fifteen, sixteen, who've decided that they're kind of attracted to the same sex and want to stand up at Christmas dinner, or at Passover, and announce it to the family.

Adam: That's not about being truthful. That's about being angry. I believe that people who say they only want to come clean and be truthful often have an ulterior motive, especially with their parents.

Dr. Drew: If you ask them why they want to do this, they say they want their parents to know them for who they are. They think being direct and honest and keeping communication lines open is extremely important. They have these feelings and why shouldn't they stand up for them? If you ask them, "Do you hate your dad?" And the answer is always, "Yeah, I hate him."

Adam: Exactly. "What would your dad's greatest nightmare be—to hear that you're gay?" And they say, "Yes, yes. How did you know?" So it's not about truthfulness—it's about a big "F-you" to Dad. Not a good reason to do it.

Dr. Drew: When your sexual identity is still developing, don't bring your parents into it—particularly if it's only calculated to make them angry. That will only put more pressure on you at a time you should be sorting things out for yourself.

The right time to come out to your parents is when you're an adult, when you're not dependent on your parents, when you've had some time to establish an identity separate from your family. It's best if you're in a monogamous relationship, so you can get support from your partner if it turns out that your parents aren't supportive.

And keep in mind: Heterosexuals do not announce to their parents when they become sexually active or that they're going to have sex. That's a needless red flag.

Most adolescents are still dependent on their parents in so many ways, emotionally and otherwise. So it's extremely uncomfortable to talk about these intimate issues.

In an ideal parental relationship, these things should be able to be discussed. Remember—the parent hopefully will be there to help the young person contain potentially destructive behavior. Performing this role properly usually is not particularly pleasant for either the parent or the child.

It turns out that parents have a window of opportunity between eight and twelve to begin discussions about sex and relationships with their children. If it isn't initiated then, they may lose them forever to their peers.

15

Abuse

Celebrity Input

★ *from Actress Jennifer Grey*

★ ★ ★ **Q: I'm a fifteen-year-old girl and my mother has been dating a man who has a son my age. One time when we were together he raped me. I didn't tell anyone because I was embarrassed. Now my mother is going to marry this man and this kid is going to be my stepbrother. What should I do? I don't want to mess up my mom's chances.**

★ **Jennifer:** Oh, my God.

Adam: Raped her?

Dr. Drew: Yeah. Now, she's got to tell Mom. Got to tell Mom. First of all, not only does Mom need to know what she is getting into, what kind of family structure she is creating, she has an opportunity to do the parenting that's going to be necessary to keep this situation healthy.

★ **Jennifer:** How about the child putting her needs ahead of her mother's needs? How about that for a concept?

Dr. Drew: She needs to.

★ **Jennifer:** She obviously must have some kind of narcissistic mother or some crazy mother.

Adam: Oh, something's up with Mom, just by virtue of the fact that she brought home a guy who has a fifteen-year-old rapist for a son. Because the acorn doesn't fall too far from the tree.

★ **Jennifer:** I think that what happens very often as kids is you are so busy trying to protect your mom, trying to protect your mother's feelings for you, that you constantly—

Dr. Drew: But, Jennifer—that's what narcissistic parents groom their kids to do. That's how the kids define themselves.

★ **Jennifer:** Yeah—take care of the parent before themselves.

Dr. Drew: Yes. It's very wrapped up in that.

Adam: You have a way of internalizing things that happen to you when you are younger, thinking it's your fault no matter how uninvolved you were.

Q: How do you define abuse?

Adam: It's tough to do that.

Q: Is spanking abuse?

Dr. Drew: Yes. There are studies that show increased antisocial behavior in kids within a few weeks of one single episode of physical abuse. Even if a child is struck only once as a form of punishment, the chances of antisocial behavior shoot up: things like lying, doing poorly in school, striking other children.

Now, I'm in favor of spanking when a child is about to hurt himself; in other words, if they're doing something that threatens their physical well-being, I don't care what the consequences of the spanking are—that behavior has to be stopped. But anything short of that is physical abuse. Corporal punishment of any type has adverse consequences.

The most powerful way to influence behavior is negative conditioning, which is not the same as punishment. Rather, it's the removal of a positive thing. Tell a child that you'll take away a beloved toy if he misbehaves and see what happens.

Q: What constitutes verbal abuse?

Dr. Drew: Very tough question. When is the normal give-and-take between a child and parent abuse? It runs a wide spectrum. To me, in a very general sense, parenting has a great potential to become abusive when it is not empathetic. Whenever there is no respect for the child as an individual who has feelings, when the parent is screaming and demeaning the child, that usually qualifies as abuse.

Q: Are there other kinds of abuse?

Dr. Drew: Abuse may be an overtly intrusive parent who doesn't allow the child to breathe or have any sort of independence. Overinvolved parenting is a subtle but obstructive form of abuse. Teenagers frequently describe how their parents prohibit them from having phone calls or wearing makeup. They won't let their kids out of the house after four in the afternoon. So it's not surprising that teenagers talk about running away from home. Kids think about running away only when there's some form of abuse. And that's abuse. When parents intrude too aggressively, that's abuse. When parents don't acknowledge the existence of their children as separate, whole human beings and are not empathic to them, that can become abusive very rapidly.

Adam: The opposite is true as well. Neglect can be abuse. Withdrawing emotion can be abuse.

Dr. Drew: Abuse doesn't have to be more than the run-of-the-mill, common quality that we hear about today, something overt like sexual, physical, assaultive, emotional abuse. It can run quite a broad spectrum. Having a parent who is an alcoholic or mentally ill—that's an abusive environment. It's an unhealthy environment and kids are commonly abused in various ways in those environments.

Celebrity Input ★ *from Actress Jennifer Grey*

Q: My father physically abused me so much that I have a real problem with anger, particularly with people who try to control me—like my boss. Any suggestions on how to manage this?

Dr. Drew: People today aren't really taught that containment is maybe a good thing to do with some of their feelings sometimes. Letting it all hang out is not necessarily a good thing. We need to be more mature about when we choose to let certain things out. And anger, particularly anger that's so dysfunctional, needs to be contained and let out in small doses and more appropriate ways. Like boxing or lifting weights, punching a heavy bag. To allow a person to let off some of the pressure.

Adam: I'm sort of with Drew, in that we make a lot of excuses for people in their actions, when in the old days we basically just told them to calm down. Now no one can be stupid anymore. They have to be learning-impaired. And no one can by hyper anymore; they have attention deficit disorder. People have to know boundaries, and just because you had some wrong done to you as a youth doesn't mean you have to see your dad in the eyes of your employer.

Dr. Drew: Now, the more serious problem is that this all is going to surface from the abuse in an intimate personal relationship, which will be impaired. So if you're concerned with creating more stability and satisfaction in those relationships, or if you are having overwhelming symptoms like depression or anxiety, then you have to pursue things like therapy. But in terms of containing anger, the message is, "Hey—contain it."

★ **Jennifer:** I think that it's so common that people experience some form of abuse early in their life. To realize that when you are older, to process it in a way so you don't constantly recreate it, is important. People who see themselves as victims have a really hard time moving through it. They wind up ignoring it or denying it. It ends up affecting your life constantly in every form. You become a victim in every situation and you don't know why it's always you.

Dr. Drew: What I've come to realize recently is that the issue of powerlessness is a paradigm in the human psyche. When children, who are so powerless, have these horrible experiences, they spend their whole life trying to find ways to avoid that.

★ **Jennifer:** Or finding ways to recreate it over and over again.

Dr. Drew: They end up acting it out. Because they see powerlessness or potential powerlessness in every human interaction. And so they become defensive and act in ways that are very dysfunctional.

Q: What are the effects of abuse?

Dr. Drew: It's simple and frightening: People who are abused become abusers or victims of abusers. If you are physically abused as a child, you will probably be abusive to your children and your mate. The same if you've seen, say, your mother being battered by your father; that's the behavior you learn, the behavior you carry with you into your adult relationships.

And people who are sexually abused as children tend to act out that same kind of attack on children when they get older. It doesn't even have to wait until adulthood. It can be as soon as preadolescence or adolescence, preying upon younger children, acting out sexually in inappropriate ways. It's an unfortunately simple equation: If you have been preyed upon as a child, you will probably become a predator or a victim. And that affects every relationship you will have for the rest of your life, unless you get some kind of treatment.

Adam: Here's an example of verbal abuse: That was long-winded and boring. Please learn to edit yourself, you a-hole.

Celebrity Input ★ *from Brian Vander Ark and Donny Brown of The Verve Pipe*

Q: I was involved in abusive relationships with a number of men so I decided to try to switch to women. But the ones I'm with also seem to abuse me. What's wrong with me that they all want to abuse me?

★ **Brian:** I think that, when there is a lack of self-confidence in someone, anyone that has a type A personality is going to take advantage of that. They'll jump on that person.

Adam: Here's someone who's been wearing that KICK ME sign for a long time. Who put the first one on her? It's usually Dad or Mom that slaps that on early and they just go through life like a petition collecting signatures.

★ **Brian:** I think that it's just human nature to actually pull up at some point and become the antagonist.

Adam: You mean the abusee becomes the abuser? What do you think, Drew?

Dr. Drew: I think that's true. People who are good victims, when they finally find somebody who can stay with them emotionally, they end up abusing them. Because it's too painful, they end up getting too close.

Adam: Sometimes they abuse them just to get them to start abusing them back because that's all they know.

★ **Donny:** It's one of the emotions that they understand.

Q: We screen potential mates for their sexual history and for sexually transmitted disease. Should we be screening potential mates for a background of being abused?

Dr. Drew: Absolutely. It's never talked about.

Adam: You mean asking them if they like Dad? That's all you need to know. You just ask one question: "Do you like your dad? Yes or no." That's how you figure out what kind of relationship you're going to have with this person and how they're going to be.

Meaning: Your wife will use her dad as the role model to abuse you or not. When you're talking about the ability to parent and the ability to be in a relationship, you've got to ask: "Where is your dad? Do you ever talk to him? How do you like him?" You could make pretty good decisions based on that. Women can do the opposite. Ask the man: "How do you like your mom?"

Q: What if you find out that the person you're involved with has been abused? Should you get out? Is that a make-or-break issue?

Adam: I'd say yes, if they're not actively seeking some kind of recovery or treatment.

Dr. Drew: That's good advice. Recovery could be within the context of the relationship; it doesn't necessarily have to be treatment.

How to Help a Friend... *who is being abused*

Dr. Drew: Contact social services. With criminal abuse, you blow the cover—you don't worry about your friendship. You don't worry about anything. You worry about getting this person safe. If they're actually being abused by somebody close—and that includes being hit with an object, someone's hand, being struck—that's criminal.

Celebrity Input

★ from A. J. Dunning and Donny Brown of The Verve Pipe

Q: I was sexually abused by my father when I was a little girl. Now I have nightmares about it when I am in bed with my boyfriend. What should I do?

Dr. Drew: We see sexual abuse as a child affect people in a couple different ways. Either they become hypersexual or they become averse to sexuality. The whole experience of sexuality triggers some very intense feelings of helplessness and powerlessness. And pain. I mean, you were violated by the most important caretaker in your life in a way that was destructive to your emotional development.

Adam: It seems to me that when this has been done to someone, it's like a unibody car getting wrapped around a telephone pole. You can straighten it out, put some Bondo on it and paint it, but it will never quite be the same. It's always going to pull just a little bit to the left.

Dr. Drew: Yes, it always is. And if something has yet to straighten out, then it's going to drive in circles. It's gonna be a big mess.

★ **Donny:** You guys make a lot of auto-body analogies?

Adam: We're opening an auto-body and upholstery shop. We'd like you guys to be there for the ribbon-cutting ceremony. So what do you guys think: A. J., Donny? Don't want to put you on the spot, but feel free to speak your mind.

★ **A. J.:** It's certainly a matter of therapy.

Dr. Drew: I wonder what is the nature of her capacity for intimacy. Is she calling some guy that picked her up in a bar her boyfriend? Or is this somebody she's been able to maintain some kind of stable relationship with? These are all ways in which abuse affects people's capacity for relations of any type. It's forever a problem. And even in long-term therapy, sometimes the best thing a therapist can do is just help people contain the psychological turmoil that's left over from these big traumas. Sometimes people can have physical relations if they are able to find a partner to kind of work with them.

Adam: I think his job in the relationship is to be as understanding and sensitive as possible. And her end of the bargain is to get some therapy. And hopefully they can meet in the middle somewhere. Or just go lesbian and call it a day.

Dr. Drew: That's why people become strippers and go into porno when they have this kind of history. They need to feel powerful in their relationships with men. It's such a helpless, annihilated feeling.

Adam: Drew will not rest until I'm back masturbating to *National Geographic*. Because of him, I don't know whether to cry or masturbate when I see this pornography—from Drew's constant brainwashing.

Q: What if you're in a relationship—with a husband or boyfriend—that turns abusive?

Dr. Drew: They need to seek treatment—or you need to leave. Professional help—or you're out the door. Once somebody, particularly a male, begins physical abuse on a female, it's only going to build. That's a line that people can't cross over.

Q: Why would someone stay in an abusive relationship?

Dr. Drew: Because that's what they expect from a man—and in a subconscious way, they elicit that. Even if they understand what's happening, there are women whose subconscious need to stay connected to this person also requires certain amounts of abuse.

Adam: There really are no coincidences in relationships. A lot of stuff seems like good luck, bad luck, serendipity, misfortune, or whatever—but people know what they're doing, at least on a subconscious level, when they enter a relationship.

Dr. Drew: But even if the woman has elicited this behavior, the overwhelming message from us is this: The abusive partner needs to be treated—or you need to leave. Even when the partner gets treatment, the woman also needs to get involved with that treatment and to change, as well.

Adam: Why leave, though, if this is what you're seeking?

Dr. Drew: Because they don't understand how severe the problem can be. They don't have a sense of what they're dealing with.

Q: What form does denial take when someone stays in an abusive relationship?

Adam: They usually talk about what a loving, great guy he is when he is not abusing them. And that's probably true. Because if you smack someone around on Monday night, you've got to be pretty good on Tuesday—you can't just be lukewarm. These guys are buying flowers, begging the women to stay. Some of these guys get real intense. There's a lot of "I'll kill myself—I love you so much. I smacked you around because I saw you looking at other guys and I'd rather take my own life than see you be with someone else."

Dr. Drew: The woman, who doesn't have any sense of self-worth, experiences that as: "God, he loves me so much he would do this." And it's just BS—he doesn't care about you at all. He cares about the leaving part because he can't stand any sense of loss, but he doesn't really care about the person. That's a relationship with no respect or empathy.

Women will describe in great detail how their boyfriends have so many flaws—they smoke pot, they try to beat them, they don't have jobs, they're toothless—and they'll have been with them for three years. They're thinking of marrying them but they're having second thoughts and they don't understand why.

Adam: What is that? That's the worst part of people. If people chose relationships the way they choose cars, we'd all be in good shape. I'm serious. You don't like those tires, you take a look at the service record—it doesn't look good, well, you don't buy the car. If guys were like cars, that one would be a '74 Chevy Vega with the stick shift knob missing.

Dr. Drew: And then there are guys who sound like two different people. A woman will say her husband has abused her—but when we address the reality of that, all of a sudden they switch off: "Oh, but he's this other person. You don't understand. He's this other guy who can be really sweet and loving. You've got him all wrong." They come to his defense. And defense is really the key. When they start defending the position that's unrelated to reality and untenable, that's denial.

Q: If you've been abused as a child, how do you keep from abusing your own kids?

Dr. Drew: Treatment—awareness and treatment. Anybody who's been abused will be at least slightly abusive to their children in some way. And even if you get treatment, it will take a couple of generations before the abuse washes out of the family.

Adam: The day you eliminate kids being raised by people who shouldn't raise kids, by people who were abused themselves, is the day you close down the prisons and cut back on the police force. That's when utopia sets in.

What to Do If You're Being Abused

If you're underage and being abused by a parent:

Dr. Drew: You have to rely on other adults. That's a hard thing to do because you don't trust adults already. I would say, first go to other family members. It's hard because the child automatically feels responsible for the behavior he elicits in the adult. So, if another adult yells at him, it just confirms his sense of being at fault.

Adam: You tend to think that whatever your childhood is, that's the way everyone's is. Sammy Davis Jr.'s kid probably thought everybody's dad was in the Rat Pack. Unfortunately, I had to watch *The Brady Bunch* and *The Partridge Family* growing up, and I realized pretty quickly that, *Geez, my life sucks. My life isn't like theirs at all.*

Dr. Drew: Most people who are being abused really don't identify it as abuse. They really don't know. They don't understand that it's not appropriate to be struck by a parent. It's not appropriate to be fondled in some peculiar way.

Even the ones who are being sexually abused sometimes can't identify how off-the-scale that behavior is.

If you're underage and being sexually abused:

Dr. Drew: If you don't have family members who respond immediately to try to get you out of the situation, the child has to go for social intervention: Child Protective Services, the Department of Social Services. Tell a teacher at school.

Q: How common is abuse?

Dr. Drew: At least the majority of people's problems is with abuse—ultimately abusive relationships.

Adam: Considering we see so many issues and yet abuse is the one issue that crops up more than fifty percent of the time, I certainly agree with that.

Q: Why is abuse so common?

Dr. Drew: Because it's based on the family—and families are imploding in this country. People who were abused become abusers or victims or both. Our culture has done very little to capture this population and help them—very little. And the people who were abused grow into dangerous adults. There's an interesting phenomenon: We have this outpouring of empathy for the abused young person. Yet that person is going to be the abuser we're condemning ten years from now. The ones we're screaming about locking up because they are abusers—they're the ones we feel horrible about if they call up as a kid being abused.

Adam: It's almost like we feel guilty as a society for not getting involved when the kid was ten or eleven or twelve. So now they're eighteen or nineteen and they pull a carjacking, maybe pull the driver out of the car and smash his head with a cinder block—let's give him nine months' probation because he was abused. We don't really say it but I think society feels sort of bad: He came from a broken family, he doesn't know who his dad is—we didn't really take care of him.

Dr. Drew: Thomas Jefferson observed that a society that loses its will to punish cannot survive. And we've lost our will to punish and contain because we're trying to be sympathetic about an abuser's history. People who have been broken, people who are disturbed—they need containment. It helps them and it helps society.

16

Narcissism and Entitlement

Q: What is narcissism?

Dr. Drew: According to the fourth edition of the *Diagnostic and Statistical Manual of Mental Disorders*—or the *DSM-IV*—it's a pervasive pattern of grandiosity in fantasy and behavior, the need for admiration and a lack of empathy toward others.

Adam: It's the guy who says: "I don't care if it's right or wrong—we're talking about *me*! I'm going to get something out of this."

Dr. Drew: It's the idea that the world exists only to serve you, to meet your needs. That no one else's feelings mean anything—only yours. Nobody makes you do anything. You ask for everything and you demand to get it because you deserve it—just because you exist.

ADAM's

Philosophy on How Not to Be a Self-Pitying Loser

Here's the way you think in life. It's kind of weird. But I know it from both ends—and I'm drawing on personal experience here:

When you look in the mirror, you either see someone who gets stuff done—or you see a person who gets stuff done to him.

If you look in the mirror and see the guy who gets stuff done, that creates its own momentum. Then you get stuff done.

And if you see the guy who gets stuff done to him, the perpetual loser, then you show up Monday and fail. That's what you do because that's what you are. You have to get tired of getting beat on.

The pain of being a loser has to become tougher to take than the pain of getting your ass off the sofa. It sucks to have to go to night school after work, but it also sucks

Q: What are the effects of narcissism?

Dr. Drew: It comes back to parenting. And our society is so poorly parented that we end up in one of two camps.

The majority of people in this country seem to feel they must have their needs consistently met perfectly. You respond to my needs perfectly or I have to destroy you or be aggressive against you. Or else you become someone who feels so crappy about yourself that you idealize everybody else and don't look at how really full of crap they are.

Adam: Let me take it a step further and say that, in terms of meeting their needs perfectly, they don't even know what their needs are.

Dr. Drew: Oh, but they do. Not consciously. Yet the needs are endless—boundless.

Q: Is narcissism common?

Dr. Drew: Narcissistic issues are very common, almost ubiquitous. The society is built around it.

Adam: People dabble in it. They can do very narcissistic things without being narcissistic.

Dr. Drew: Narcissistic behavior is extremely common; narcissistic disorders are the psychiatric disorder *du jour;* they've become that common. Each decade has its dominant trend. Narcissistic disorders clearly are the ones right now.

making fifteen thousand dollars a year. Which is worse?

Q: What are the most common relationship problems related to narcissistic behavior?

Adam: I guess the most glaring example of that is this sort of thinking that the other person is there for you in the relationship. So you should do what suits you, what you want to do, not necessarily taking into consideration what they may want, whether it's physically or emotionally or even just what movie you're going to see that night.

Dr. Drew: Abuse usually is due to narcissism—and vice versa. Narcissistic disorders allow people to abuse other people because they don't really acknowledge the emotional existence of other people. They don't feel it.

Q: How are narcissism and abuse-related narcissistic disorders related to entitlement?

Dr. Drew: Entitlement is the message that our society gives people which allows narcissism to go on in a flagrant state. Narcissists feel quite justified in taking their position because society tells you you're entitled to everything.

Adam: I think narcissism says you're entitled to everything—and then society doesn't really stop you.

Dr. Drew: Society confirms it: "Go for it. It's yours. You go, girl! It's all yours. Take it!"

Adam: If you really wanted to distill it down, it gets into welfare and a lot of other government-related subjects that end up supporting that idea.

Dr. Drew: Absolutely. Government supports it top to bottom. It comes back to our sense of guilt. We feel guilty and empathic—and we end up making choices that support the ill health, rather than move people in the direction of health.

Adam: The reality is that the definition of health is to pipe up when it's time to pipe up and to keep quiet when it's time to keep quiet. A lot of people have difficulty with that.

It takes a really well-adjusted person to be able to stand up when the time is right and say, "Hey, wait a minute, this won't do. This isn't right." And it takes a pretty adjusted person to lie back and say, "All right, maybe I screwed this one up. Maybe you have a point."

Celebrity Input

★ *from Actor David Alan Grier*

Q: My parents expect me to be perfect. Perfect grades, perfect around the house, perfect weight. What should I do?

★ **David:** Every parent wants their child to be perfect. The one thing I really loved and respected my mom for was that I knew she expected me to get the best grades I could in school but she never hassled me. She demanded it but in a silent sort of way. Anytime a parent or peers demand perfection or you demand it of yourself, things can go wrong. I know that when I was in college, a lot of those kids, the straight-A students in high school, were the first to crack up.

Adam: There's a balance between doing good for you and doing good for them. The parents' job is to coach you into doing good for you.

Dr. Drew: When parents demand that you do something because it's really for them, they're nullifying you as a person. That's abuse. It's empathic failure. Whenever you're not acknowledging the other person's existence, you're being abusive. Even if you're not being overtly, physically abusive, you're being abusive. Now you've got someone whose whole sense of themselves is wrapped up in pleasing you. They never develop any sense of themselves. They'll either rebel against that or they'll try to be perfect for you. In either case, there's going to be some sense of a lack of empowerment, a feeling of being out of control, a lack of sense of self and a narcissistic sort of defense has to develop around them. That's a recipe for an eating disorder.

Q: How do you define entitlement?

Adam: That you feel you've got to get what you want to get.

Dr. Drew: Right. You're entitled to everything. You're entitled to win the Lotto—because Grandma down the block won.

Adam: Here's the way I would approach that. Go ahead and think you are entitled to everything. But keep in mind: So is everyone else. Therefore, you're all entitled to something, or you're all not entitled to anything.

Realize the person you're talking to thinks he's entitled to everything, too. Maybe everyone is. Let's just say the glass is half entitled. Yeah, you deserve everything in life—but your neighbor deserves everything, too.

Dr. Drew: It's about the balance between individual and community.

Adam: What people have to realize is this: Life is not about what you can get away with. That's the way too many people approach it: Let's see what we can get away with. Let's see how far we can go before someone tells us to stop.

Dr. Drew: Because nobody else exists. Nobody except us and our needs.

Adam: But no matter what you get away with, you can never get away from yourself. You can cheat and steal and murder—and never, ever get caught at any of them. And that just means your life was the life of a cheat, a thief, and a murderer.

Q: How common is entitlement?

Dr. Drew: Every child now grows up with a sense of entitlement. That's what the media and the government pump out. Kids are five and they have a sense of entitlement.

Adam: Well, it's a little harder to escape now. If you grew up in the rural South around the turn of the century, what the hell did you know about what's going on in other parts of the country or the world? Now, all you have to do is turn on the TV to realize what you don't have.

Dr. Drew: TV is telling you what you should have.

ADAM on How Society Works

Society is basically a beehive. Here's how a beehive works:

It's a bunch of bees, taking care of business. The hive's main goal is to get honey for the hive. They're busy.

Once in a while a rogue bee will fly away from the hive and sting you on the ass for no reason whatsoever. It's the equivalent to some guy chucking a rock through your living room window because he was drunk and felt like it. By and large, it doesn't happen.

Now you get a ghetto-blaster cranked up and put it on your shoulder and go walk under the hive and smack it with a stick and, yes, the bees will turn on you. They'll chase you right into the lake like a bad Yogi Bear cartoon.

But if you dress like a normal human being and get in there and start gathering honey, they'll welcome you into the hive—or at least they won't pay any attention to you. And if you start collecting more honey than the rest, you'll suddenly be the queen of the hive.

Adam: It's telling you, "You live in a world that's one hundred percent go-get-it!"

Dr. Drew: Most people today are raised in a nonempathic environment, where you're not taught to have empathy for other people. So you have no reason not to walk up to someone and just take what they have—

Adam: —to just take someone's sneakers.

Q: So what are you entitled to?

Adam: I think you're entitled to basically get back whatever you put in. I mean, if you're a cheater, you're not really entitled to anything. If you're an abuser, you're not really entitled to anything. If you're a decent, caring, nurturing, honest, loving individual in a relationship, then you're entitled to that right back. I don't think you could say everyone is entitled to love and nurturing if they're getting drunk and abusing their partners.

Q: Can you give an example of entitlement and narcissism?

Adam: For a guy, it's: "I'm having sex with my girlfriend and I want to have sex with her friend and her sister at the same time. Why not? It's what I want to do. It's my penis we're talking about and, after all, you only go around once, blah blah blah."

The women's version of that usually is: "I like this guy but I like his best friend, too. My guy went to his uncle's farm for a month during the summer and I got together with his friend." When we say, "Well, you've got to tell this guy," the response is, "I don't want to lose him."

"All right, so stop seeing the other guy."

"Well, I really like him."

And this is what little kids do. When one kid is playing with a toy and sets it down and another kid picks it up, the first kid grabs it back because, even though he's done playing with it, he doesn't want anyone else to have it in case he wants it back again.

Dr. Drew: Well, narcissism is a primitive personality type—

Adam: That's what I'm saying. Sorry for cutting you off, but *I* want to speak now.

Dr. Drew: You *go,* girl!

Adam: Every child is basically that way. A kid's eating his snack; he looks over at your snack and decides he wants that, too—so he takes it. It's up to the parents to say, "No-no-no. You can't have that." We need that no-no-no.

Dr. Drew: The next level is to understand how you would feel if someone did that to you. But we haven't even gotten to the no-no-no level. We don't even tell people, "That's wrong!" It's like, "Yeah, go for it!"

Adam: All that Reebok advertising: "This is your world. Go for it." Meanwhile, it's the parent's job to slap the hand. If the parent is smoking reefer, talking on the phone when the kid is doing this,

ADAM and DR. DREW

on Narcissism and Delayed Gratification

Dr. Drew: The inability to delay gratification feeds into narcissism because people really don't identify anything other than their immediate needs—their own needs.

Adam: We live in a society that needs such balance—between delayed gratification and instant boner. But everything is fast now. It's funny that society keeps becoming faster, because basically what faster is about is gratification.

Meaning: I'm hungry and I want to eat now. So instead of going out to the barn and slaughtering something and picking this and boiling that and firing up a woodstove, we've got a microwave.

Dr. Drew: And a freezer and a convenience store around the corner.

Adam: We live in a society where faster is better and we have to keep moving faster. On the other hand, not taking the time to put on a condom before you get it on is going to come back to haunt you.

Dr. Drew: We grow as humans only by delaying gratification, by taking the more painful route. We would all rather take the path of least resistance. But the path with the greatest payoff ultimately is the one that is the most uncomfortable and difficult to do up front.

Just to grow emotionally, you have to learn to feel and work through painful things. Rather than avoiding painful things and creating defenses against them—which is getting back to narcissism—you have to actually feel the pain, experience it, be genuine and truthful and connected to reality

Adam: So what do you do? What is life? Okay, here's what life is:

Hey, the stuff that tastes good makes you fat and gives you heart attacks; the stuff that tastes like shit is good for you. That's all you need to know.

Eat the stuff that tastes like shit most of the time. Then go ahead and reward yourself once in a while by having chili fries.

then the kid gets used to not being disciplined. Then, if he sees a pair of sneakers in some kid's gym locker, he figures, *Why not?* and takes them. And society does nothing—until the kid is eighteen. Then, when we catch him doing this, we say, "Now we're locking you up. We're going to put you in jail now. We didn't get to you early and try to help you out with all this stuff—but now we caught you and we're tossing you in jail."

Q: How do you get past that kind of behavior?

Adam: Well, for one thing, we need people to stop having kids. End of discussion. Forget about nighttime basketball, forget about clean-needle exchange programs, forget about more prisons. We need people to come from good families.

Which means, basically: Everyone, stop having kids for a while. If you can stop screwed-up people from having screwed-up kids, it would take care of the problem in a generation or two.

17

Alcoholism

★ *from Kevin Coleman of Smashmouth*

★ ★ ★ **Q: How can I tell if my dad is an alcoholic?**

Dr. Drew: If you are worried, if your relationship with your dad is affected by his use of alcohol, then you're probably dealing with an alcoholic. Alcoholism is defined as progressive use in the face of consequences. If there are other family members with alcoholism, and he is having some mounting consequences, then you probably have the disease.

Adam: I think if you have to ask that question, there may be a problem.

★ **Kevin:** Especially with so much information out there today. I mean, just turn on *Jenny Jones* once a week and you'll have a show on addiction. It's pretty easy to figure out your dad's an alcoholic. It doesn't take Sherlock Holmes to figure that one out.

Q: If you have a family with a history of alcoholism, how likely are you to be prone to it?

Dr. Drew: If one or both of the parents have the disease, the probability per child of inheriting the genetic predisposition seems to be about 50 percent.

Q: If you see that as a pattern in your family, how do you keep yourself from becoming one?

Dr. Drew: If you find yourself having consistent and increasing problems with alcohol, and you're aware of that family history, you have to avoid alcohol. Basic as that. Because if you continue your relationship with alcohol or other addictive substances, your momentum will carry you into that addiction as well—your brain reward centers become conditioned to the alcohol, and eventually you won't be able to control it.

Q: Is it as simple as that? Or are there other factors?

Dr. Drew: One of the main factors that pushes young people into using alcohol is the attempt to escape from negative feelings. "I'm bummed out—having a drink will help me feel better." But the young person with a family history of alcoholism, as much as possible, needs to learn how to cope with those feelings on his own, so he won't come to rely on substances to make them go away. You have to learn effective coping skills as a young person; if you start using alcohol—or pot or another substance—to get rid of negative feelings, you don't develop emotionally. You never learn those coping skills and so, if you try to quit drinking at thirty, you still have the emotional development of a teenager. Also, when you start drinking as a teen, the actual structural development of the brain is arrested, further blunting the capacity for emotional development.

ADAM says: You Should Probably Cut Back on Your Drinking If . . .

- Miller Time for you is just before breakfast.
- Recycling day at your house is a bonanza for the homeless.
- You keep a keg tap on your key ring.
- You throw up every day—and you're still gaining weight.
- The triplets you went out with last night were actually one girl.

Q: How do you define alcoholism?

Dr. Drew: Alcoholism is a genetic disorder with a biological basis. It's characterized by a progressive preoccupation with drinking and continued drinking in the face of adverse consequences. And denial.

Q: Now—define those terms.

Dr. Drew: Progressive preoccupation: In other words, that's what you end up thinking about all the time. You plan your day around alcohol and make deals with yourself about how and when you're going to use it. It becomes a priority in your life.

Use in the face of progressive consequences: I'm talking about serious consequences on relationships, at work or school, your legal status, your finances, your health. You've already had two DUI arrests, but you keep drinking and driving. You're in a relationship and the person you're with has warned you that if you keep drinking he's going to leave you—but you keep drinking. You've been warned about showing up at work after drinking—but you keep drinking and going to work. Those are all progressive consequences: jail, loss of a relationship, loss of a job. But you're still drinking.

And denial: In other words, despite all evidence—you've lost your job, your wife, your driver's license—you still refuse to believe you have a problem. "That wasn't because of my drinking; I just had a run of bad luck." Bad luck—caused by your drinking. "I can control my drinking." Well, no, you can't. But you're in denial.

Q: Is binge drinking on the rise?

Dr. Drew: A little bit more. That tends to go through cycles. I think we're back in one of those again, where heavy binges are popular. Many of the universi-

MYTHBUSTERS

Myth: *Alcohol is not a drug. Or: Alcohol is not as bad as cocaine because it's legal.*

The truth, according to Dr. Drew: Alcohol's effect on the brain is pharmacological, as much as any drug. In many respects alcohol is worse than other drugs of addiction because it acts as a poison to all human tissue. It destroys brain tissue, damages the liver, and makes alcoholics more susceptible to cancer of the head, neck, esophagus, and colon. Alcohol suppresses immune function and causes a severe form of addiction called alcoholism. The addiction tends to be slower in developing than some of the other, more addictive chemicals, such as heroin or cocaine, but the disease that ultimately develops is just as severe as any other form of addiction.

ties we've visited have had to develop very stringent alcohol policies in response to this trend.

Q: Why?

Adam: Drew, you may have missed this part of life. But where I grew up, most of the guys, when we were all sixteen, seventeen, especially twenty, twenty-one, there was some boozing going on—and it was about quantity. And the guys who said no were ostracized.

We had a drinking game we played with big shots of tequila—and one of the guys who was losing might have eight or ten shots into him and not be in any kind of shape at all. If he lost again, we told him to take the shot—and if he didn't do it, it was a big deal. If someone said, "No, I've had enough—that's my limit," he was roundly attacked. There was a lot of peer pressure—not only to get drunk but to really drink excessively. It was almost like a rite of passage.

Dr. Drew: I've been through that, too. When I went to college, the drinking age was eighteen and drinking was the core ritual around which we organized our weekends.

Adam: That's interesting. I wonder why it didn't take.

Dr. Drew: But we should also point out that this kind of drinking is what leads to alcohol poisoning and people dying because they drink too much in too short a period of time. There have been several highly publicized cases in the last couple of years where kids at frat parties have died because of exactly that pattern of drinking: where they drank so much so quickly that the alcohol actually killed them. That kind of binge drinking may be popular, but it's also dangerous.

Q: How can you tell if you're drinking too much too often?

Dr. Drew: When you start having consequences from your drinking. When you start to lose things: a relationship, a job, a car. And your family history.

Q: What's the difference between abuse and addiction?

Dr. Drew: It takes time for the addiction to develop. But abuse can be very dangerous, too.

For example, people who drop acid ten times are not going to become addicted—but they can have some serious biological consequences from that. Doing ecstasy or drinking until you go into a coma—that's abuse, as well as being potentially fatal. When you drink or do drugs until you have a seizure, or you pass out and aspirate vomit, that's abuse. Particularly with young people, abuse is more the issue than addiction in terms of risk to their health.

MYTHBUSTERS

Myth: *I can't become an alcoholic if I drink only beer.*

The truth, according to Dr. Drew:

It doesn't matter how you drink your alcohol—addiction can occur. Whether you're drinking beer, hard liquor, or mouthwash, exposure to alcohol is the important element. An alcoholic's consumption will increase over time, even with long periods of sustained abstinence. Without treatment, the overall progression will be toward greater alcohol consumption. If one prefers the drinks with a lower concentration of alcohol, the individual will simply drink more.

Celebrity Input

★ *from Rapper-Actor Ice T*

★ ★ ★ **Q: Is it true that you can get really loaded really fast if you use alcohol enemas?**

Dr. Drew: Why does it always come back to the butt humor when Ice T is around?

Adam: He's a magnet.

★ **Ice T:** I have absolutely no knowledge of enema techniques.

Adam: Come on, Ice, sure you do.

★ **Ice T:** For real—I don't know nothing about them. I know people do it to get off, but I don't know nothing about the action, you know, enema bags.

Adam: Hey, Drew, do you absorb alcohol quickly there?

Dr. Drew: Yeah, you do. You can absorb it quickly, and it can be kind of scary, because you have no way of assessing how much you are getting. And people can get large doses rather quickly.

★ **Ice T:** You can stick alcohol into an enema bag? If you stick it in, wouldn't it sting or something?

Dr. Drew: Yeah, it wouldn't feel good, but I think it would be absorbed. I don't know the rate at which it would be absorbed. But I'm certain it will be absorbed through the colon.

Adam: Drew, if you took a forty-ouncer and just put it on there like it was a Sparklette bottle on a cooler, would bubbles come up out of it? Would it drop down a little bit?

★ **Ice T:** Alcohol in an enema bag.

Dr. Drew: This is not a great question.

Adam: Well, it's not a good question if you have a mouth.

Dr. Drew: Or a brain.

Adam: But as long as you have another orifice that you can pour alcohol into, this is the last resort.

★ **Ice T:** But I'm just totally unfamiliar with the whole enema thing to be totally honest. I know people do it but I don't know a lot about it or why.

Dr. Drew: It's a very absorptive area if anything liquid goes in.

Adam: And I guess the question is how much faster do you absorb it this way. I'm guessing people do this because they don't want to drink a bunch of hard liquor.

Dr. Drew: They don't want to vomit.

Adam: This is why wine coolers were invented: so you wouldn't have to put bottles in your ass.

Q: When does abuse cross over into addiction?

Dr. Drew: When it continues to progress in spite of consequences. Adam and I were talking about alcohol abuse: We would sit ritualistically with our male peers and abuse. There was no momentum so the problem with drinking didn't evolve beyond that for us.

Q: What should you do if you realize that your drinking is getting out of your control?

Dr. Drew: If you're abusing, you stop. You choose to stop. That's what abuse is: You can start or stop. But even with abuse, you've got to acknowledge that you're putting yourself in harm's way.

If you can't stop, if you've progressed to the point where there's an addiction at work, then you need outside help, whether it's Alcoholics Anonymous or another twelve-step program. Because, as I've said, it's not just about the drinking itself but the factors in you—genetic, emotional, and otherwise—that lead to the drinking. Therapy can be helpful as well, because more often than not the drinking is a means of covering up bad feelings you don't want to deal with, at least initially. It's not enough to stop drinking; you also have to find a way to cope with the feelings that will make themselves known when the alcohol is no longer available as a tool to mask them. It just so happens that the twelve-step process is specifically designed and perfectly suited to this task when done properly.

MYTHBUSTERS

Myth: *Alcoholics are simply weak. Not drinking is just a matter of willpower and they don't have enough.*

The truth, according to Dr. Drew: Nothing could be further from the truth. As I work with alcoholics and addicts, I find them to be a very intelligent, rich, and strong group of individuals. But they have a genetic predisposition to this addiction, which makes it easier for them to start and harder for them to stop.

DR. DREW on the Biological Effects of Alcohol

Alcohol is a poison to all human tissue. It causes it to age prematurely; cells stop producing proteins and doing the work they're designed to do.

It is particularly harmful to cells that do not reproduce, such as the central nervous system. As a result, alcohol causes a progressive degeneration of the central nervous system: memory loss, dementia. Alcoholism leads to a greater inability to tolerate frustration and causes sleep disorders and mood disturbances.

It also can cause the degeneration of the peripheral nervous system, with effects such as numbness and burning in the feet. As I said, these are cells that can't reproduce themselves; once the damage is done, it's permanent and irreversible. It damages the nerves that control sexual function, causing difficulty in achieving erections or orgasm. Interestingly, this is the one piece of information that makes an impression on young males.

Alcohol damages tissue and organs right down the line, from brain to toes. A few examples:

- The immune system is suppressed to the point that alcoholics commonly die of pneumonia. Alcoholics also tend to be at higher risk for tuberculosis.
- Alcoholics tend to get cancers of the mouth, tongue, throat, larynx, and pharynx—particularly alcoholics who smoke.
- Alcohol can destroy muscle, most important the heart muscle, ultimately leading to heart failure.
- The small intestine, key to absorbing nutrients from food, is easily damaged by alcohol and loses that absorption ability, causing nutritional deficiencies.
- Alcohol damages the pancreas, causing it to digest itself.
- Alcohol also damages the liver; the damage results in swelling and scarring—cirrhosis—reducing the liver's ability to clear the blood of waste products.
- Alcohol results in increased risk of bladder, prostate, and colon cancer.

18

Drugs

Celebrity Input

★ from Writer-Director-Performer Keenen Ivory Wayans

★ ★ ★ **Q: My husband used to be an alcoholic. He hurt his knee playing softball, and after he had arthroscopic surgery, he started taking Dilaudid and he won't stop. What should I do?**

Adam: What do you think you would do, Keenen, if this was your partner? I guess it's not different from getting hooked on any drug, really.

★ **Keenen:** What she has to realize is that he's not hooked just on painkillers. He obviously has an addictive personality and if it was alcohol last time, and painkillers this time, there is going to be something else next time. She has to get him into treatment—that's it. Because the next excuse that he gets, he's going to get addicted to something else.

Adam: You hear about the stories from Elvis on up that there's been a lot of celebrities hooked on a lot of stuff that was prescribed by a lot of doctors and it still did them in. Just as fast as heroin or coke would have.

★ **Keenen:** More people in our business die from the legal stuff than the illegal stuff.

Adam: So don't treat it any differently than if it was any other drug.

★ **Keenen:** No, don't just treat the drug. You've got to treat the person. This guy obviously has a problem.

Dr. Drew: Dilaudid is a very powerful opiate, like heroin. And opiates tend to cause the most profound form of addiction. It is rapidly progressive. People on opiates have the most severe difficulty remaining off their drug, particularly in their first year. You need to get your husband to an addiction medicine specialist and get him into treatment as soon as possible.

He needs to be detoxified in a medical setting. He needs comprehensive addiction treatment and this is something that usually requires very intensive, long-term treatment, like two weeks in a hospital followed by at least twelve weeks of follow-up. If he doesn't want to look at this, you either A) leave, B) go work on your own codependency recovery, go to something like Al-Anon, or C) develop something called an intervention, which is where you get all the important people in that person's life together. And for men, the most important, the most powerful element is actually the employer: Bring them together with an interventionist, and rehearse the intervention to actually deliver an ultimatum that they must get to treatment or you must be prepared to leave that person's life. There you go.

Q: Which drugs seem to be on the rise?

Dr. Drew: That depends. Pot has been very popular for quite a while now. LSD goes through many cycles, but is much more popular now than I would have imagined.

Amphetamine is huge now. I would have said that amphetamine would never overtake cocaine in popularity, since cocaine is a much more addictive drug. But because amphetamine is so cheap, so available, so well-distributed, it now is overtaking cocaine. Also amphetamine is an antidepressant, so people start using it somewhat therapeutically at first, to help them feel better, work better. If they're smoking pot all the time, eventually they'll get depressed—and amphetamine lifts them right out of that depression. When the pot stops working, the amphetamine takes over—eventually with even worse effects.

Adam: We don't hear that there's a hot new drug out there that's sort of sweeping the country. It's all on pretty equal footing these days—although I would say cocaine is definitely down while speed is up.

Q: How do you know if you need rehab?

Dr. Drew: You need recovery at the point at which you feel you have had significant losses and can't stay stopped.

Adam: Don't you need it when you can't quit drugs?

Dr. Drew: Not necessarily. Most people don't come into treatment until they're on their knees begging for help because they lost lots of things and have tried to maintain it themselves and can't. If you have a family history of addiction or alcoholism and you are accumulating losses, you need rehab. Are you going to get it? Probably not until you have substantial loss. Ideally, people would identify the problem and get help before they had too many losses.

Adam: Don't people attempt to stop by themselves? Nobody goes right to rehab, do they?

Dr. Drew: But that's the point. Addiction is progression in spite of consequences, whether it's drugs or alcohol—because the pattern is the same for both, and having a history of alcoholism in your family makes you susceptible to other kinds of substance addiction. In fact, it underlies more than 85 percent of addiction.

Consequences make you want to stop. But even if you try to stop, it progresses. You know you better stop drinking but you can't. Dad, Grandpa, Grandma—

everybody was an alcoholic and you realize, *I've got a problem here. I can't seem to stop.* Except that, at the age of fifteen or seventeen, they aren't that clear about it. It's only later, when they've killed three people in a drunk- or drug-related driving accident and they've been fired from three jobs and they have liver disease and can't make any relationships work—it's only then that they realize they can't simply do it their way and stop on their own. Hopefully, someone doesn't have to progress this far before they seek help.

Q: What can you expect from rehab?

Dr. Drew: First of all, it's a safe, structured environment where you can be away from whatever the substance is you've been trying to stop. There'll be a medical detoxification—if that's necessary, depending on what the drug is. You'll be encouraged to bond with a group of people with the same disease. And you'll spend your days in groups, discussing important emotional material.

Some of that has to do with discussing how the substances have affected you, the losses you've accumulated, and how you're going to deal with that. You may also talk about the basics of how you're going to organize your life, to create a structured environment where you can survive and stay sober. As time goes along, you'll ultimately start discussing those emotional issues that made you want to escape into drugs or alcohol in the first place. Typically, they're issues of abandonment and powerlessness.

You'll learn to grow and mature through relationships with peers with a similar illness, through the twelve-step community. You'll work with a sponsor, someone who has been through what you've been through, who can help you make honest assessments of who you are and what you are, so you can be as honest as possible about how you're put together. At the same time, you'll learn how to structure your life in a way that excludes substances.

You'll also learn as much as possible about the disease of addiction—and make no mistake, it is a disease. In rehab, you learn a lot about it because you see the same disease and hear the same stories over and over again in other people; no matter who those people are, the disease affects everyone in the same way ultimately. Remember the polar bear theory.

How to Help a Friend... *who's getting involved with drugs*

Dr. Drew: First you have to sort out whether your friend is experimenting with drugs or just acting out with them, or whether he's potentially an addict. Family history will tell you a lot about that: If somebody has an alcoholic in their family and they're experimenting with drugs, there's at least a 50 percent chance of addiction. If your friend is an addict who is in denial about their drug use, one of your jobs is to confront the person with the consequences and try to break through their denial as much as you can. But realize that they may reject you as a friend.

You don't have to be an addict to have a drug problem. If you're dropping LSD once a month you've got a drug problem. People damage their brains with hallucinogens. If your friend is doing that, you're justified in notifying an adult to help a friend so they don't harm themselves.

Adam: It's like you've committed a crime against yourself and you've just relinquished rights. People feel a little apprehensive, that it seems uncool to tell someone. But how would you feel if you didn't tell anyone—and then your friend got strung out and wasted five or eight or ten years of his life? I've seen it happen in my friends. Being a friend isn't just about telling people what they want to hear and having a good time all the time.

Dr. Drew: Being a friend can be very unpleasant. Just like being the parent, it's not about being the buddy. You've got to do what's best for the person, selflessly, regardless of what it does for you.

Adam: It ultimately may not help the relationship.

Dr. Drew: But you'll help the person, and that's being a friend.

Celebrity Input

★ from A. J. Dunning of The Verve Pipe

Q: My friends all smoke pot but I've tried it and I don't like it. I don't know what to do to tell them I don't want to do it when they all get together for one of their all-night sessions.

Dr. Drew: Why do you have to tell them anything?

★ **A. J.:** Exactly. A person has a right to choose what they wish to do. If it's a question of peer pressure, then maybe you're running with the wrong group of people. If it's not a question of peer pressure, if it's just a question of wanting to do the right thing for yourself, then you just have to be more assertive in saying no.

Adam: I think it's a pretty tall order to ask fifteen- or sixteen-year-olds to say, "I'm sorry, that's not for me. I don't choose to. I'm saying no." Ultimately you start defining your group and your clique by commonality. I mean, that's why guys in the band hang out together and guys on the football team hang out together. You share common interests or there are common things you don't like. Ultimately this is just part of the defining of your group.

Dr. Drew: Except, Adam, like people who have alcoholic parents, people who themselves are not alcoholic tend to be drawn to alcoholics. And it may not be that it's about him choosing that kind of behavior, but he is still drawn to people that participate in that kind of behavior and he has to acknowledge what that means about himself. He's not going to change them, but that's sort of what his focus is. If they smoke pot and he wants to be around people who smoke pot, then he should hang out. If he doesn't want to, he should leave. Someone once said, "Show me your best friend and I'll tell you about yourself."

Q: How many times does someone have to go into rehab before recovery works?

Dr. Drew: That depends on the drug. Relapse can be part of the disease. Usually after they've been through a course of treatment, the party is over. The difficult part of addiction is that it's one of the few diseases where the doctor has to convince the patient A) that he has a disease, and B) that he needs to take treatment. Denial is part of this disease, and that's what health-care professionals must fight to get people to recognize the relationship between their addiction and the consequences they've suffered.

Treatment is cumbersome and time-consuming. But the consequences of refusing treatment are profound.

MYTHBUSTERS

Myth: *Some drugs are only psychologically addictive.*

The truth, according to Dr. Drew:

The term "psychologically addictive" shouldn't even exist. It may describe why people begin a relationship with substances, but not why they become addicted. Addiction is a disease, a biology that operates when people use substances despite their willful desire to stop. A substance is either addictive or it's not—and if it's addictive, it's because it operates at a primitive biological need that has little to do with someone's psychological need to escape from an unpleasant emotional state.

Q: The so-called war on drugs has been going on for almost twenty years. Yet rates of drug use continue to rise. Are people that unable to deal with their feelings?

Adam: I think we're living in a society that's based on addiction. If you take a look at a lot of the advertisements, they talk about "slamming" a Mountain Dew or "pounding" a stack of Pringles. When they show a guy drinking a Pepsi or a Coke in a commercial, he doesn't take a few sips and put the rest away for later. Everything is about chugging something. About consuming something like a shark.

Madison Avenue has turned snacking into an extreme sport. It's all part of that instant gratification thing: Get it done and get it done now. Even when it comes to working out, you don't just work out—you get pumped! You can't just sit down and eat and then take a nap anymore: You've got to slam down your food, chug down your drink, and then take a power-nap. Everything's got to be done with this aggression.

Dr. Drew: It's all about thrills and immediate gratification. Everybody wants a thrill from everything.

Adam: Everything is about this kind of thrill: Get yours, get it all, do a lot of it. When you see a car commercial, the guy driving the car isn't stuck in traffic or obeying the traffic laws—he's out on the open road, the stereo cranked up, and he's just sailing through a canyon somewhere. I mean, drugs is the next logical step.

Dr. Drew: Here's my feeling on that. Thrills are a way of making yourself feel better. If you feel empty and devoid of real meaning in life, it's a good way to fill that up. Because it does take you away from it for a few seconds—because we've lost the notion that our interpersonal relations and gratification are what cause us to feel good as human beings. We can't tolerate any frustration.

Our primary relationships—with our parents, siblings, and children—are all screwed up. Our families never give us the nurturing consistency we need to feel good about ourselves. So the only way you can have any sense of relief and gratification is with an immediate thrill. Our ideas of parenting have lost sight of the fact that children must learn to deal with frustration and life's shortcomings, rather than avoiding or denying them.

And not only are people who are devoid of meaning in their life prone to be gratified by thrills—if they have the biology of alcoholism underlying that, then the need for thrills develops momentum because of that, because thrills activate the mesolimbic reward system, the same part of the brain as alcohol and drugs. Then you have increasing difficulty doing without it.

When you look at alcoholics and other addicts, they tend to be gratified by thrills in ways that nonaddicts aren't. If you ask a roomful of addicts what they would do if a bomb were to explode nearby, the overwhelming majority of them would say they would run toward the bomb

MYTHBUSTERS

Myth: *Marijuana is not addictive.*

The truth, according to Dr. Drew: Marijuana is not addictive to many people but it can be, to a subset of people, primarily alcoholics. That is to say: people with parents or grandparents who are alcoholics, who themselves have had momentum with alcohol, can very easily become addicted to marijuana. The symptom is absolutely characteristic and reproducible.

It takes about three exposures to marijuana before an individual actually experiences the high from the drug, almost as if the brain needs to be primed before the euphoric effects of the drug. Around that third exposure, someone who is predisposed to addiction will have an extraordinarily positive experience. They will love the effect of the drug, feel it is one of the best things they have ever experienced, and from that day forth will be preoccupied with pursuing the drug. They may not use every day but they will think about using every day. That intense desire to use will go on for somewhere between one and twenty years. At the end of that time, the euphoric effects of the drug tend to wear off and people start to become increasingly depressed, irrito see what was going on; they would be attracted by the thrill and excitement. Where the majority of nonaddicts would run the other way.

You get caught in a cycle where you can never get out of that because the biology makes you continually pursue it. You never get the chance to get off the merry-go-round to try to develop some stable relationships because it's just not as rewarding or gratifying. Relationships also become a way of pursuing thrills; God forbid they should be frustrating.

table, forgetful—the marijuana doesn't work anymore. You'll hear people say they stopped because they didn't like it anymore—and they will usually transition to another drug, typically speed and/or alcohol.

ADAM reveals: Things a Pot-smoker Shouldn't Do After Lighting Up

- Start that diet you've been putting off.
- Watch a "NOVA" special on reproductive anatomy.
- Pluck your eyebrows.
- Begin your singing career.
- Program your new VCR.
- Change your pennies at the supermarket.
- Read the ingredients label on a Twinkies wrapper.
- Fixate on the headlights of oncoming cars.
- Break out the banjo.
- Watch a second "NOVA" special: "Tapeworm: Friend or Foe?"

ADAM and DR. DREW on Marijuana: Pro vs. Con

Dr. Drew: The case for the legalization of marijuana is compelling. It does not appear that the occasional use of marijuana—on the weekends or once a month—harms anybody. The problem with pot is it is addictive, particularly in people who are prone to alcoholism.

Adam: Give me a pot-oholic over an alcoholic any day of the week. I have friends who, when they drink, they're aggressive, boisterous, sexed up as hell—and when they get stoned, they just curl into a ball. I believe as a society that it's the guy who is drinking who is out getting aggressive with women. I want to see statistics about guys who rape while high on pot. I would say I would have an easier time raping someone when I was stone-cold sober than I would when I was high on pot. I can't even get off the f-ing sofa to get to the fridge when I'm stoned—how am I going to rape someone?

Dr. Drew: The marijuana addict will tell you they love the drug. They remember the first time they got high; it was usually the second or third time they smoked pot. And they wake up every day thereafter thinking about that drug.

Adam: Drew, you've been reading too many books.

Dr. Drew: That's not in any book. That's my own personal observation. There are also biological reasons, particularly for people under the age of eighteen, not to smoke pot. People's brains are still evolving rapidly until the age of fifteen or sixteen. That development can be damaged; the evolution of their brain can be blunted by exposure to pot or other drugs. Parts of the brain are overstimulated in abnormal ways and cell connections disconnect. As for the argument that pot is natural: Plants and animals develop these chemicals as a defense mechanism; it's meant to harm you to keep you from destroying the plant.

Adam: I'll still take someone who smokes pot over someone who drinks any day of the week. They're less hostile, less aggressive, and more laid-back.

Dr. Drew: I have to agree with that—and I remember when I signed on to that philosophy with you. It was when Cypress Hill was on the show and they were four years into their promarijuana crusade. They were smiling, passive lumps of flesh.

Adam: Lambs. Little lambs.

DR. DREW on Recreational Drugs and Their Effects

Cocaine: Cocaine is a phenomenally addictive drug, although it is primarily people with a tendency toward alcoholism who become addicted to this drug. It is generally used as a powder, which is snorted through the nose, or in a crystal form, which is smoked. It can also be melted and injected intravenously. Smoking the drug—what used to be called freebasing and has now been distilled to crack—produces almost instant addiction. The drug is a powerful stimulant, one that causes a rush of energy, a feeling of power and euphoria. The medical effects of sustained use include constriction of the blood vessels to the kidney and heart, restricting crucial blood flow to those areas.

Cocaine was originally developed as a topical anesthetic, to be rubbed on a surface to numb it; it was also found to constrict blood flow. So it was decreasing both pain and surgical bleeding; but when used recreationally, that tendency to cut blood flow means it constricts or closes crucial veins and arteries in the brain, the kidneys, and the heart. So extensive cocaine use can lead to kidney failure, strokes, heart arrhythmia, and heart attacks. Long-term use also leads to extreme paranoia and delusion.

Amphetamines: Amphetamines are stimulants that increase the heart rate and blood pressure, causing one to feel more awake. They also tend to suppress appetite. Amphetamines can be taken in pill form, snorted, or injected. Though addiction is usually slow to develop, the effects are severe. They include extreme paranoid delusions and hallucinations, usually that people close to the user are out to harm him. This can have devastating effects on relationships and can lead to violence. Because they increase blood pressure, amphetamines cause excessive stress on the heart. They also appear to alter mood centers in the brain, and may create an effect akin to a small stroke.

Ecstasy: A close relative of amphetamines that has been synthetically altered to give it hallucinogenic properties—sort of a combination of amphetamines and LSD. While it conveys a euphoria and energy, it also creates paranoia more rapidly. It has been shown to cause central nervous system damage, with side effects that include delirium, as well as a kind of catatonia, with people becoming stiff, unable to move, confused, and delirious.

Marijuana: Marijuana is smoked or eaten and causes euphoria and giddiness. There continues to be debate over its medicinal property, such as for the relief of glaucoma pressure within the eye, the control of nausea in chemotherapy patients, and the increase of appetite in AIDS patients suffering from wasting syndrome. Used regularly, however, marijuana can be addictive, almost exclusively in persons prone to alcoholism. Long-term marijuana use can have significant effects on short-term memory, as well as causing irritability, depression, and a lack of motivation. Frequently, someone who has become addicted to marijuana will find himself unable to achieve the euphoria he associates with using the drug and will switch to amphetamine, which can cause an even more serious and consequential addiction. There is also evidence that people using marijuana before the age of eighteen, before their brain has finished developing and evolving, run a serious risk of damaging that development, creating the potential for long-term mood disturbances and emotional problems.

Hallucinogenics: This is a category of drugs that includes LSD, ecstasy, morning glory seeds, mushrooms, peyote, and PCP. These drugs cause hallucinations, as well as feelings that can range from intense euphoria to equally extreme paranoia and even psychosis. These drugs generally are ingested, in pill or dehydrated form, and tend not to be addicting. But they present danger in another form, in that the person taking them can never be sure of the quality or dosage he is ingesting. They can cause brain damage, particularly when taken by someone under eighteen, by destroying cell connections in the brain that have yet to evolve. The most common effect is chronic mood disturbances and personality changes. There is also the possibility of an effect called post-hallucinogenic perceptual disorder, in which the hallucinations, the sense of detachment and unreality caused by the drug, do not subside after a normal period but hang on for up to a year; this can be associated with severe depression.

Opiates: Derived from poppies, these drugs cause a severe form of addiction. The drugs in this category include heroin, morphine, opium, methadone, and such prescription drugs as codeine, Percodan, Demerol, Percocet, and a number of others. Opiates are depressants, used primarily as painkillers. They can be ingested, inhaled, smoked, or injected. The intravenous method presents its own deadly side effects, with the potential of everything from overdose to contracting the HIV virus by the use of contaminated syringes. The addiction is a particularly strong one, causing both difficult withdrawal and a subsequent feeling described by former users as a persistent feeling of emptiness or loss. Though they do not cause brain damage, opiates, particularly used intravenously, can lead to other health problems, ranging from lung, heart, and kidney diseases to nutritional deficiencies.

Inhalants: Inhalants can cause brain damage, particularly inhaled hydrocarbons. These include glue, paint, and gasoline. Nitrous oxide—usually obtained from performance car shops or propellant units in whipped-cream dispensers—causes euphoria but can also cause a psychotic state, resulting in hallucinations and paranoia. Nitrous oxide, which is used as an anesthetic, can also cause a shutdown in the peripheral nervous system, basically resulting in a paralysis that begins at the feet and works its way up the body, until the individual cannot breathe without the aid of a ventilator. It can be both life-threatening, and occasionally permanent. Amyl nitrate is an inhalant that causes sudden, brief euphoria—but this is probably as a result of decreased oxygen to the brain. While it may cause euphoria, it also can cause potentially permanent brain damage, caused by that depletion of oxygen to the brain.

19

Psychological Problems

Q: What's the difference between anorexia and bulimia?

Adam: Anorexia is not eating at all. Bulimia is eating a lot and then vomiting. A lot of people assume that anorexia is involved with it.

Dr. Drew: Because it's usually anorexia/bulimia, which is the more common manifestation. They go together very often—people will go back and forth, manifesting both, one, or the other.

Q: Is this strictly a syndrome among women? Or does it happen to men as well?

Dr. Drew: It does. It's much less common, but it does happen to guys.

Q: How do you tell the difference between someone with an eating disorder and someone who's just on a strict diet?

Dr. Drew: According to the *DSM-IV,* the criteria for determining whether someone is anorexic include refusing to maintain a minimally normal body weight—usually to the point where you weigh less than 85 percent of what you should for your age and height. There's also an intense fear of gaining weight or becoming fat, even though these people look like skeletons. They're in denial about how serious a problem their low body weight is because they're totally focused on their weight and shape—that's completely how they judge themselves. But they have no perspective; they may look emaciated, but when they look in the mirror, all they can think is, *I'm too fat.*

For bulimia, the symptoms include binge eating, followed by some form of purging: self-induced vomiting or misusing laxatives, enemas, and diuretics. To be classified as bulimia, this would be happening twice a week or more for three months. And, like the anorexic, this person is totally unrealistic about their weight and what they actually look like. They can never be thin enough.

Adam: Here's the deal: It's all degrees. Everybody has an issue with food. I don't know anybody who doesn't. I don't know anyone over the age of twenty or twenty-five who gets a big thing of banana cream pie and doesn't announce to the table, "I shouldn't be doing this."

One of my loves in life is going out to a nice meal. If I know I'm going out to a nice meal that night, I'm looking forward to it from three in the afternoon, until I get to the restaurant. Then I eat too much and then I feel a little badly and swear I've got to run it off tomorrow. Those are issues. I think everybody has them, but it's a matter of degree.

Dr. Drew: When do personality traits become a disorder? It's the same issue.

Adam: Right. Because having issues with food is kind of a good thing—in moderation. Otherwise, you just eat pie.

Celebrity Input

★ from Actor Jon Cryer

Q: I've heard that using laxatives is a good way to lose weight. Is this true?

★ **Jon:** Boy, it's not. Am I right, Dr. Drew? I mean, you're the doctor.

Dr. Drew: You will lose weight but by causing your body to get dehydrated. All the laxatives do is cause stool to move through the colon quicker so no water is absorbed out of the stool. But you still absorb the same number of calories. You get electrolyte imbalances. You can get a problem with your bowel motility. You can get kidney abnormalities such that, when you stop the laxatives, you'll start retaining fluids at an extraordinary rate. Your legs will swell up and you can have heart problems and arrhythmia. The problems can be profound.

★ **Jon:** And you'll always have a panicked look on your face.

Dr. Drew: It's part and parcel of an eating disorder that just by itself carries a terrible prognosis. About 20 percent of people with bad eating disorders die. And it tends to be a chronic and progressive problem. Don't do it.

Adam: Listen, any time you fool your body, it's a temporary solution, but ultimately losing weight is about not eating like an idiot and getting a little exercise. That's it—everything else is a temporary fix. You can fool your body for a little while and then it ends up screwing you up.

Q: What are the long-term effects of these eating disorders?

Dr. Drew: Things like softening of the bones, osteoporosis. The ovaries shut off and the menstrual cycle stops. There are heart disorders, all sorts of disorders of the gastrointestinal tract.

Bulimia tends to be more dangerous. The medical consequences are phenomenal, profound. For bulimics, who are vomiting frequently, the stomach acid wears the enamel off the teeth. Your skin changes, your hair changes and can fall out—and you can permanently damage your colon with laxative abuse. The bowel just stops moving, fills up with stool, and never moves again. Sometimes they need digital extraction of the stool. Or even surgical removal of the colon.

Adam: You mean it just goes on strike?

Dr. Drew: It stops moving.

Adam: When you say digital extraction, you're not talking about using a computer.

Dr. Drew: No, with fingers, with digits. I've seen people who have had to have their colon removed. It just goes on and on. There's a 20 percent fatality rate in bad bulimia cases.

Adam: You know, you can screw around with your earlobes all your life. You can smoke some cigarettes for a while and get away with it, drink a little booze on the weekends, and be okay. But one of the most fundamental processes of the body is to take food in, get what the body needs out of it, and get rid of the excess. When you start messing with that, you're in big trouble. When you do this, it's like fucking with the engine room on a big ship. You're just going to be drifting with the tide. Screw that.

Dr. Drew: In our society, women particularly are prone to complain about their weight and trying to achieve some perfect appearance. Society pushes women to do that.

Adam: The problem is that, a lot of times, what you look like, how much you weigh, has to do with heredity. There's nothing you can do about it.

Also, food is always so attached to your psyche that, when the psyche goes off balance, the food always gets affected. Some people get real compulsive about what they eat. Some people stop eating. Some people compensate by eating too much.

Dr. Drew: A person with an eating disorder is the opposite of the aggressive, acting-out person. This is someone who acts out against him or herself, who is so pissed at her parents that she acts out in this primitive, subconscious way.

To some extent, this is another kind of narcissism: the closet narcissist, someone who feels she has to be perfect—the only way she can feel good about herself is by being perfect. They tend to be overachievers, to idealize others. The person with an eating disorder sees her job as trying to live up to the rest of the world. In some ways, it's a person who feels this is the only way she can have control over her world, by having that kind of control over her eating. It's a way of avoiding genuine painful feelings.

Celebrity Input

★ from Comic Caroline Rhea

★ ★ ★ ★ ★ **Q: My mother thinks I'm too fat and has started me using diet pills. How long should I use them and what are the side effects. Will I lose weight?**

★ **Caroline:** Lose it until you are thin enough to regain your strength to kill your mother.

Dr. Drew: Yes, exactly.

★ **Caroline:** What kind of a mother is that?

Dr. Drew: With the latest round of disasters from diet pills, I am really against them. I did prescribe fen-phen reluctantly. At one point in the midst of that frenzy, fifteen minutes wouldn't go by that somebody wouldn't walk into my office and literally demand it. People don't understand there is no free lunch in nature. If you mess with the brain chemistry to the point that it suppresses appetite, there has to be a consequence.

★ **Caroline:** The only way you are going to lose weight is to take responsibility for yourself.

Dr. Drew: In terms of health, a dietician can help you lose weight and you will lose it effectively but in a healthy way.

★ **Caroline:** Get your jaw wired shut.

Dr. Drew: But this is always the beginning of an eating disorder.

★ **Caroline:** I have the opposite of anorexia: I think I'm thin. I'm in a big support group; we all sit around in skintight clothes, passing Twinkies.

Q: Can you talk a little about your own experiences with obsessive-compulsive disorder, or OCD?

Dr. Drew: In my case, it took the form of hyperachieving. I developed that as a way of dealing with the depression I was feeling in high school. That's the only way I could feel good about myself. By the end of high school, I discovered, "Oh, this feels good." So I put a huge Band-Aid on my mood because I could deal with my feeling of worthlessness and deal with the mood and be preoccupied, all at the same time. And I could get lots of strokes from my environment without ever dealing with the genuine issues. A personal connection might have healed it, but I was too busy hyperachieving.

Adam: You know, I don't trust people who are hyperachievers.

Dr. Drew: You shouldn't. Super-hyperachievers are usually the people with the eating disorders and the overinvolved parents who never give the individual a chance to develop at all. So you have no coping skills, no sense of self. You feel worthless and you find other things you can control.

Adam: So your depression made you hyperachieve?

Dr. Drew: First it made me dysphoric: unhappy, unable to sleep, obsessive-compulsive. A mess. Then I discovered I could hyperachieve and that felt a little better. But it was still a way to avoid depression.

I'm still OCD a little. But if you can channel it, if it's not a defensive, automatic reaction to your emotional world, it can be very useful.

But OCD can be so intrusive and overwhelming, there's some evidence that links the genetic potential for addiction with OCD. They probably have groupings of genes they share in common.

Q: What are the symptoms of OCD?

Dr. Drew: According to the *DSM-IV*, there are a number of criteria for diagnosing OCD. Generally, you have persistent, recurring thoughts or impulses that are intrusive and inappropriate, that cause you distress or anxiety, such as the idea that your world will collapse unless you follow your rituals. So you develop mechanisms for suppressing or neutralizing those thoughts. Things like snapping your fingers a certain number of times—or being afraid to turn the TV or radio off on a negative word and doing it only on a positive one. Or maybe you're convinced that the number three is somehow magical or necessary in your daily routine—you feel you have to touch the doorknob three times before you open it. Or you must wash your hands three times. And you develop all of these rules and behaviors to keep those fears at bay, rituals that can consume hours a day and interfere with your normal life, your relationships, your job.

Eventually, you'll begin to recognize how this behavior controls your life, that you've become a slave to these obsessions and compulsions. But usually there's nothing you can do to control it without seeking professional help.

Q: Is there a relationship to drug use?

Dr. Drew: OCD is a biologically based disorder, a defensive structure against threatening feelings.

I believe that marijuana can induce OCD. This isn't a medical opinion, just something I've determined from my observations. I don't know if people who are obsessive-compulsive are more apt to be marijuana addicts, but certainly once they become marijuana addicts, they tend to be very obsessive-compulsive, in terms of intrusive thoughts and ritualistic, repetitive behavior that they feel they have to perform or something bad will happen.

Adam: I don't know. I think pot cures obsessive-compulsive behavior.

Dr. Drew: Maybe for a while. Maybe that's the point. Some obsessive-compulsives need chaos around them.

Adam: If you're going to be obsessive-compulsive, at least be a neat freak.

Q: How is it treated?

Dr. Drew: There are medications that treat it very effectively. OCD has certain psychological theories about where it comes from. I think of it as a defensive mechanism in people who are biologically prone to it. Again, it's nature vs. nurture.

Adolescents tend to get a lot of OCD symptoms. That's part of a loss of a sense of omnipotence that a lot of young people feel. OCD is a way of trying to deal with an environment in which you feel powerless. But then, so is religion, if you think about it: developing those rituals to try to control the weather and floods and earthquakes. Occasionally there's a miracle and everybody talks about it for a thousand years.

Adam: That's such a bizarre thing: people who believe God is looking out for them. "Oh, I have to have my leg removed because of cancer—God must have a plan." Yeah, His plan is He wants you confined to a wheelchair. Hey, you can't get the DMV to return your registration on time—and you think God's got a plan for you.

20

Piercing and Tattoos

Q: What are the psychological implications of extreme body decoration and piercing?

Dr. Drew: People who have what I call aggressive piercings have probably been physically or sexually abused. It's usually there.

A couple of piercings now are the style. But people with the more bizarre genital piercings—those people have issues. They've survived some kind of abuse.

ADAM Bad Ideas for a Tattoo

- Your ATM PIN number
- A recipe for gazpacho
- Your New Year's resolutions
- Your SAT score
- A picture of Kathie Lee Gifford

Or it's a form of mastery over previously perpetrated abuse: "I'm going to abuse myself before anyone has an opportunity to abuse me more."

Q: Is piercing and tattooing also a form of rebellion?

Dr. Drew: There's definitely a piss-off-the-parents quality to it: "You care about me so much? Well, screw you—I'm gonna mess up my own body."

Adam: Many a fifteen- or sixteen-year-old will say, "I want to get my navel pierced."

Why? "Because my friend has it. I think it looks cool and sexy."

How do you get along with your folks? "I hate them."

What do you think your dad will think of getting your navel pierced? "He would hate it."

Dr. Drew: More often—or just as often—it's someone who says they got a genital piercing and eventually admits, well, yeah, they were sexually abused as a child.

Adam: They have to have been. They absolutely have to. You cannot volunteer to have a spear put through your penis and not have that be the case. And I've seen this done. I mean, a spear going down the urethra and popping out behind the head of the penis is, to me, unthinkable. I would rather get in a car accident. It's almost bizarre.

Dr. Drew: *Almost* bizarre?

Adam: What I'm trying to say is, if you'd never heard of this before, you would think, "What the f— are you talking about? That's impossible. No way." It smacks of something wrong and whether people don't want to admit it and claim it's all a matter of style and attitude—we always get down to the fact that something is seriously up with these people. There's some other problem at work there and it usually has to do with abuse in their past.

Dr. Drew: People like to say, "Hey, it's a trend. It's cool." And we accept that. But too often people don't look beneath at the motivation and the symbolism, to really examine what makes people do this stuff to themselves.

★ from Steve Harwell and Greg Camp of Smashmouth

★ ★ ★ **Q: Will getting my penis pierced increase either my sexual pleasure or my girlfriend's?**

Dr. Drew: Not that we've heard of.

Adam: Not at all.

Dr. Drew: It certainly may decrease the effectiveness of normal condoms. You have to buy condoms that are specially reinforced at the tip. It seems to me there could be things that could happen like infections that could ultimately affect your ability to have sex and be comfortable. Generally, if it's not infected, if it's an otherwise normal piercing, it doesn't do anything for the guy that I can see. Women variously report that it's a good or a bad thing. Generally it's sort of neutral.

★ **Steve:** The penis pierce is something that you either—

Adam: —listen, I've seen this procedure done and it is as brutal in person as it is on the radio.

★ **Steve:** You've had it done?

Adam: I've seen it done.

★ **Steve:** Oh, okay. Jesus, Adam, you scared me.

Adam: It is as bad in person as it is on paper. Believe me.

★ **Steve:** It just doesn't look healthy. I've gotten my penis caught in my zipper and that's all the pain I really want to experience.

Adam: Steve, I'd put it this way: For me, keeping sharp things away from my penis is a full-time job. I wake up each morning thinking how I can keep sharp things away from my penis and I go to bed on my stomach thinking that thought as I fall asleep. To intentionally put your penis in harm's way, well, it's almost negligent. But the point is: Don't try to tweak your sex life that way. All these sorts of gags and gimmicks, they may be good a couple of times around, but as soon as the novelty wears off—

★ **Steve:** You're stuck with something.

Adam: You're stuck with something. And whatever it is you are stuck with, that becomes what the norm is a year from now or even two months from now.

★ **Steve:** Exactly. The penis is a delicate enough organ that it's like, why stick something through it?

Adam: It's sacred. If your body is your temple then your penis is certainly your confessional, or the altar. You wouldn't just go up to the altar and desecrate it that way. This is your most important piece of navigational equipment.

★ **Steve:** Just leave it alone.

Greg: You know that penis-piercing thing sounds kind of painful to me. It's like, you get enough pain down there sometimes with what goes on in the bedroom, so why would you want to?

Adam: And there is no anesthetic they use for this procedure. To me, if there was ever a time you were going to pull out the anesthetic, this would be the time. You can be numbed to have a wart removed on your big toe; tell me you don't need to be numbed for this procedure. But they don't do it.

Q: Do different piercing locations mean different things?

Dr. Drew: A post through the tongue is saying, "I engage in oral sex."

Adam: "My tongue died for your sins. I endured this pain for you." You know she's into oral sex. Now that doesn't mean *you're* getting a blow job. But someone's getting a blow job.

Dr. Drew: The nose is just style. So is the eyebrow—but it's style with an attitude, like maybe there's a genital pierce there, too.

Adam: Here's what it's saying: "I'm not a deeply religious person. I'm no virgin." Because no virgin has a bone through her neck. It's also saying, "I'll put up with a little pain for a little pleasure."

Dr. Drew: It's an expression of hostility and anger. It says, "I've been f—ed with—so I'm going to f— myself before someone else does. I'm angry and I'm sexually active." And the hostility, aggression, and sexuality go together.

Adam: It's saying, "I'm making a statement." And anyone who's making a statement with their appearance, I don't trust. In any kind of way. I just don't.

Dr. Drew: Because there are no free-will statements. These are all caused by something else, some psychological process. The statement isn't, "I'm free to be me." If you're making a statement in this way, it's because you've got other issues and you're anything but free from them.

Adam: It's ironic that the so-called free spirits—the people who are the most tattooed, have the craziest hair, the most holes punctured in their skin—the people who use all this to show how free they are really are slaves to the people they're rebelling against.

Q: With tattoos, are there deeper meanings than the images being tattooed?

Adam: I don't trust anybody with multiple tattoos—or multiple piercings, for that matter. I've not found a person that I would want to go camping with who had multi-tattoos.

Dr. Drew: Historically, tattoos were associated with antisocial personalities. I used to say that frequently and I would get attacked for it. And, indeed, there really isn't as much of an antisocial personality with this anymore—but there's an antisocial quality to it, a kind of "Screw you, society. I'm doing my own thing."

Adam: But the reason tattoos, long hair, scraggly beards, piercing, whatever it is—the reason this stuff has been associated with antisocial behavior is because that's where it started.

Dr. Drew: Even today, you can bet that those people have an outward aggression, as much directed outward as inward. The aggression they direct at messing up their bodies is also directed outwardly at society and other people.

Adam: Whether it's acted on or not makes no difference. If I was walking down a dark alley, would I rather run into someone with a lot of tattoos or someone with no tattoos? Give me the one with no tattoos every time.

Dr. Drew: People with tattoos and piercings and long hair shouldn't expect society to embrace them and welcome them into the higher levels of success.

Adam: I don't think they expect that. That's part of it.

Dr. Drew: But I hear that all the time from people with tattoos or piercings: "But they're discriminating against me. What's the big deal about how I look?" I had an experience with a guy recently who was a former gangbanger. He still has a braid down his back, tattoos, earrings, the works—and he's all pissed off because he can't get his kids into an elite, private school because nobody takes him seriously. Can you imagine that? Well, no one takes him seriously because he looks like he came right from a motorcycle rally. He's probably a decent business man and a great guy—but he still carries these symbols on him that people react to.

Adam: And symbols mean something. That's why they're called symbols. Here's the deal, you idiots: When you put this costume together, you do it to make a statement. And the statement is: "Stay the f— away from me. Don't hire me. I've pre-f—ed myself." It's like saying, "No one will steal my car because I broke the windshield and painted it brown." Well, yeah—but you're still driving around in a brown car that looks like shit.

Q: What if you find that kind of piercing and tattooing sexy in someone else?

Adam: I don't think you could unless you were programmed the way they are. I wonder if you're healthy if you find that attractive. I doubt you will if your head is screwed on straight. But if you're coming from that mind-set, I suppose it could be.

Q: How permanent are tattoos?

Dr. Drew: They can be taken off very easily now with lasers.

Adam: Very easily?

Dr. Drew: Very expensively, but very easily.

Adam: Expensive doesn't mean easy.

Dr. Drew: The laser treatments cost a fortune. They give you five minutes of that laser for several hundred dollars. They can do a couple of square inches per session. So it takes a long time.

Adam: So it can cost you a thousand bucks to get rid of a small tattoo.

Dr. Drew: It volatilizes the ink. It dissolves it. Pretty much all colors now.

Q: Are there places you shouldn't get tattooed?

Adam: On your liver.

Dr. Drew: In the kitchen.

Adam: Your liver. His kitchen.

Dr. Drew: In terms of places on the body, I can't think of any offhand. Tattoo artists can tell you that. They do it on genitals, inside the mouth—they do it everywhere.

DR. DREW on the Health Risks Associated with Piercing and Tattoos

With both piercing and tattoos, we worry about blood—specifically things like HIV and hepatitis B and C being transmitted through the use of unsanitary utensils and by the blood itself. There are other forms of hepatitis that are also blood-borne. That's still a rare event, but it's amazing that it's as rare as it is, given the amount of piercing and tattooing that's going on.

With tattooing, you should always be sure they use a sterile, disposable kit. When they say HIV is transmitted by dirty needles, they're not just talking about intravenous drug use. A reused tattoo gun needle can be just as dangerous as a dirty syringe.

What worries me is that in most states people need no licensing or special training to do piercing. Most reputable places will have an apprenticeship of some type for a year or two, but that's not required by law in most places.

Now, I couldn't put a needle in somebody's arm without six years of medical training. When I do it, I have to have malpractice insurance. There are all kinds of state regulations to determine when I do it, where I do it, how I do it.

But these guys can put hardware through the most sensitive, dangerous parts of the body and nobody bats an eye.

I mean, I'm a physician—and I would never pierce someone's tongue. Because there's an artery there and I would worry about nicking it. Most of these places will shine a light through the tongue before the piercing to find that artery—but they could still nick it. And if they do, the tongue could swell up to the size of a grapefruit, block the airway and cause the person to stop breathing.

Rejection is possible with piercing. Sometimes, when it looks like a piercing is infected, it's actually just an immune reaction to the foreign body. The navel and the eyebrow are the two most frequent places for that to occur.

Infections are not uncommon. If the infections become severe, they can create something akin to the flesh-eating bacteria, which people are so worried about. Well, guess what? That's how you get it—you pierce a body part and bacteria get in.

And the proximity to the brain with these infections scares me. If you have a neck infection, it goes right to the brain. Brain abscesses, meningitis—we're talking about potentially very serious medical problems.

21

Depression and Suicide

★ ***from Rapper-Actor Ice T***

★ ★ ★ **Q: I have a friend who has started acting very depressed and occasionally talks about killing herself. How can I tell if she's serious? What should I do?**

Dr. Drew: If you're not a doctor, you are not in a position to assess whether somebody is serious or not. You have to take it all seriously. But there is nothing much that you can do other than to keep them safe, keep structure around them, call the appropriate people if there are people to be called, like parents or even police if somebody really has the plan. Otherwise just be available, be around the person. That's about all you can do.

★ **Ice T:** I agree. People don't usually talk about suicide. It's not something you play with. People will maybe quickly talk about killing somebody else. I know people who are always talking about killing somebody. "I'm gonna kill them," you know, whatever. But if somebody ever says to you, "Oh, I'm gonna kill myself," bets are off. This is serious.

Adam: That's right. When somebody says, "I'm thinking about killing myself," all bets are off and it's your job as a friend to make the phone calls or do whatever it's going to take and to take it as a serious threat. It's like a bomb threat at the airport. Even if it's some teenager laughing, you still have to do the procedures. It has to be taken seriously because it's a life or death situation.

★ **Ice T:** I agree. I grew up around a lot of tough cats and they always were talking about killing somebody. You know: "Oh man, I'm gonna kill that guy." Yeah, like, whatever. You ain't gonna kill nobody, so shut up. But suicide is serious. If somebody plays with it, my next question would be, "Man, you're bullshitting, right?" "No, I'm not." Once you know they're serious, you've got to try to get to somebody and get it handled quick because you don't ever want to dare anybody to do some shit like that.

Q: What are the symptoms of depression?

Adam: To me, depression is an all-encompassing pain that makes you want to withdraw and not participate in life. Which creates more depression because there are consequences to the withdrawal.

Dr. Drew: It's a biological state of the brain where you lose any sense of worth or enjoyment in previously enjoyable things. And the manifestations are sleep disturbances, anxiety or panic, paranoia, sadness, crying and agitation, appetite changes, eating too much, eating too little, a sudden drop in grades. Sleep disturbances typically include sleeping all the time—or waking up in the middle of the night and not being able to go back to sleep. The symptoms of depression occur differently in different people. Sometimes you don't even acknowledge it as depression. When I was in it, I didn't feel sad—I just felt desperate and anxious.

Adam: That's how I felt, too. I had my moments of sadness.

Dr. Drew: And you're already so depressed—routinely, day in and day out—that you don't really notice, "Am I depressed or not?" because you can't be objective. If you tell a depressed person they're depressed, they say, "No, I'm just anxious."

Adam: You might admit to being sad, but you wouldn't admit to being depressed.

Q: How much of depression is psychological and how much is chemical?

Dr. Drew: I have to believe that with any human behavior it's a mix of nature and nurture. If you really are not biologically disposed, you're not going to get depressed. But for some people, a slight influence will trigger a depression. If you don't live a pristine life—and who the hell does?—you'll get depressed.

Adam: Is it possible that, emotionally, you get depressed, and that creates the chemical end of it?

Dr. Drew: Look, we're just a biological gel. So, ultimately, it is a biological process—the experience of it—but is the cause a gene that turns on? Or is it some inciting influence from the environment?

Adam: As someone who has been horribly depressed in his past—

Dr. Drew: I've been very depressed when I was younger, too.

Adam: I've been more depressed. Don't make me start crying here. As someone who is fairly content, fairly happy now, I know that a lot of my depression had to do with the fact that I wasn't doing anything I wanted to do and I wasn't doing anything that was gratifying. When I was digging ditches for a living or cleaning carpets, you're damn right I was depressed. You'd be depressed, too, if you went to Tony Roma's at eleven P.M. and stayed there until five in the morning cleaning a greasy carpet and got thirty-five bucks for the effort.

What I'm saying is a lot of it is what you're doing. I know there are people who are depressed; there's a chemical problem and that's that. But I think most of the people would be snapped out of their funk, if, all of a sudden, they were living their dream. Most guys would snap out of it if, all of a sudden, they were doing Claudia Schiffer and owned a Ferrari dealership.

The problem is, it's a horrible cycle, because they get depressed because they're not doing anything gratifying. That slows them down even more and then they become unable to pursue or put the energy into doing what they want to do, which ultimately seems to take a lot of energy.

Dr. Drew: Not being able to do what you need to do and not being able to identify your needs are part of what happens with depression. If you don't have any connection with your real emotional needs, it's pretty hard to get them met. So you won't be able to figure out what you need and be able to make choices.

Very often, the real cause of our depression was the lack of genuine relationships. Depressions tend to be about loss or being isolated and alone.

Adam: For me, my depression was never around a connection. Therapy was helpful for me, but fighting through the depression and achieving and doing what I wanted were the greatest relief for my depression.

Dr. Drew: Competency gives you the skills to go and do the things you need to.

Adam: So here's the point: I'm happy now and I was horribly depressed then. I knew I had to do that to get to where I am now.

Q: Is talk therapy preferable to chemical treatment?

Adam: Yes, of course it is. I think there are too many drugs prescribed. We hand out pills in place of hard work a lot of the time.

Dr. Drew: Depression can motivate you to make changes and do the things that, hopefully, will make you better.

Adam: It takes work not to be depressed. You're lying on the sofa, you feel like you're seven hundred pounds because you can't get up. But you get your ass off the sofa, you put on your running shoes, and you go out and run three miles. And when you come home, you feel better.

Dr. Drew: I believe, too, that we overdo the medication. Still, there are plenty of psychiatric conditions that really are medical. There are some great medicines and they can be used in conjunction with talk therapy. But real change, the real move toward fulfillment, is hard work. And you need to remember that seventeen million people suffer from depression, and 17 percent of them die from it. Medicine is an important part of controlling the illness.

Young Drew: *This is Drew, fifteen, from Pasadena and I was just wondering is it normal for guys to think all the time about people in the media or movies, things like that, people on TV?*

Adam: *Of course. That's why they get paid all that money. That's why they're on the cover of the tabloids and all that stuff.*

Dr. Drew: *It's normal for fifteen-year-old females to do that; in fact, it's sort of encouraged. Is this a male or female you're obsessed with?*

Young Drew: *It's a female, somebody in the movies. And I really want to meet her. I just keep thinking about what it would be like to know her and just kind of hang out with her.*

Adam: *Who is it?*

Young Drew: *Do you know the movie* The Exorcist*? It's the girl in that.*

Adam: *Linda Blair. She's quite attractive. Did you see the movie?*

Young Drew: *Yeah, I saw the movie and it really affected me. It kind of happened at a time when I was already sort of upset. I had just been with some friends up in the mountains and we got lost and almost died. So it was amazing that we went to see that film right after having been through that experience.*

Adam: *First off, let's look on the bright side now. You're not stalking the priest so you're relatively healthy. Do you have any plans to contact her? Have you ever done anything, ever wrote her a letter?*

Young Drew: *No. How would you even go about this? I wouldn't even know what to say. Are you telling me you could set me up with her?*

Adam: *No, I'm trying to squelch that. I'm just saying, have you ever made any sort of attempt to contact her?*

Young Drew: *No. I just think about her all the time.*

Adam: *What's missing in your life?*

Young Drew: *I don't know. What are you talking about?*

Adam: *Here you are focusing a lot of your energy on Linda Blair but you're fifteen. You could be dating girls your own age, or girls who would talk to you.*

Dr. Drew: *Mood disturbances are real common at this age. You get depressed and that's why you're preoccupying about this girl you can't have. It's less painful than dealing with reality, which is being ineffectual with your peers, not being happy generally.*

Adam: *He didn't say he was depressed.*

Dr. Drew: *It's true. But this call suggests a low-level depression. It's really lacking the ability to use reality and real peers to manage. To engage in reality and truthfully address things in a way that's gratifying. Stay focused on your school, Drew: College is more important than any of this crap anyway.*

Adam: *Yeah, and I say you shift your focus where I shifted mine: Adrienne Barbeau.*

Young Drew: *Oh, yeah, I watch her all the time.*

Adam: *That's where you should be focusing.*

Q: How does depression relate to abuse?

Dr. Drew: People who are abused tend to be at a higher risk for depression.

Adam: Thanks, Moms. Thanks, Dads.

Dr. Drew: It's very difficult to feel good about life itself if you've been violated by the people you love the most. It's a real loss of self and other relations. It's hard to have a trusting relationship with anybody if your primary relationships were abusive.

Adam: Who are you going to trust when your dad smacks you around? Imagine what that instills in a person. Here's the guy who's supposed to take a bullet for you and he's beating you up or feeling you up. Why should you trust the guy on the street?

Dr. Drew: It's impossible to heal those things. You can't make the connection with people you need to make connections with in order to get better, in order to develop. It's very isolating, very depressing, very stressful—and stress makes people depressed.

Q: How is depression related to drug use?

Dr. Drew: What are the reasons that people use drugs these days? The primary motivation of drug use is escape. They want to escape bad feelings.

But most of the drugs people use to escape or elevate their mood result in long-term biological depression. LSD, ecstasy, marijuana—they all predispose the brain to depression. Any regular use of hallucinogenics before the age of fifteen or any use over, say twenty or thirty times, can result in chronic severe mood disturbances.

Q: What are some of the other effects of depression?

Adam: Well, there's a certain degree of desperateness involved with being depressed: "The pain can't get much worse so I might as well do a lot of stupid things. Because what do I have to lose?"

If it's something that has to do with a relationship—usually the end of a relationship—it can lead to a little stalking, a little getting drunk and barging in. When you really don't give a shit, you figure incarceration or a hospital stay is not such a bad alternative to the pain you're in at that moment.

What I used to do, because of my depression or sense of self-worth: I never took any kind of safety precautions with anything. I rode my motorcycle in the rain with bald tires. In my early days in construction, I would hop right up on some scaffolding hanging over a roof and have a saw in my hand and start cutting away. Because I felt like what did I have to lose?

Q: What can you do about it?

Adam: You can't push through it. You can't fight it. You just kind of weather it when it's coming on like a freight train. Later on, you see if you can chip away. People look for a quick fix when they're depressed: If I could just score with the right woman or buy the right car or hit the lottery.

That's the mistake of our society. Our society consciously says, "Buy a lottery ticket and see if you can sidestep depression." Like that's going to make you happy.

Serious depression means you seriously don't care. And here's what your job is when you don't care: You have to somehow act like you *do* care. Don't kill yourself. Don't kill the woman or man who won't take you back. Try not to get arrested or get an addiction or maim yourself. See if you can keep from getting fired. If you can keep from doing any of those during the six months when you're really bottoming out, then you'll get better.

Dr. Drew: The fact is there are worthwhile people out there and you can connect with them if you stop blaming the world. People tend to get over depression by connecting with other people. We basically develop our emotional world by connections with other humans. That's how we become who we are. That's why things like the twelve steps work, because it's saying, "Drop the BS. Make an inventory and connect with people who have the same problem. Work with a sponsor and you'll get better." And you know what? They get better. That's how therapy works.

Adam: My definition of mental stability is being all right when you're alone. I'm not talking about getting along with other people, or being able to have relationships, intimate or otherwise. It's just being okay with being quiet and on your own. I'm talking about just being left alone with your feelings and not having them turn on you. Not having to drown out those voices in your head. But that's why we have the kind of constant stimulation we find in the world today—whether it's MTV or video games or drugs or whatever. It's all about distraction. That's why, the more screwed-up you are, the louder you like your music.

Young Adam: *I'm thirteen and I don't know what to do. My mom spends a lot of time by herself in her room. I'm worried about her.*

Dr. Drew: *Where's your dad?*

Young Adam: *My parents got divorced about five or six years ago and he lives a few miles away.*

Dr. Drew: *Any siblings?*

Young Adam: *A sister. She lives here, too.*

Adult Adam: *What if you just knocked on her door and told your mom to get out into the kitchen and rattle those pots and pans? What do you think she would do?*

Young Adam: *I don't think she'd do it.*

Dr. Drew: *Does she ever make you breakfast in the morning?*

Young Adam: *No.*

Dr. Drew: *Here's the deal. Your mom might be overwhelmed with caring for you and your sister. It doesn't mean she doesn't love you; it doesn't mean she's not concerned about you. It's really difficult for a single mom to manage everything.*

Adult Adam: *What's going on in your life, Adam? How do you do in school?*

Young Adam: *Bad. I can barely read, I can't write. I get lousy grades.*

Adult Adam: *Is there anything you do that takes your mind off this? Something you're good at that you enjoy in spite of everything?*

Young Adam: *I'm good at sports. I have friends and we like to ride our bikes and our skateboards and play sports.*

Adult Adam: *Well, Adam, listen, you're not always going to get what you need from others, not even your parents. Doing well in sports is good, having a lot of friends is good. If you could do a little better in school and get the hell out of there, go off to college somewhere, you could get out of there in a few short years and let Mom fix Mom.*

Q: Why is teen suicide on the rise?

Adam: I don't suppose we could blame it on Marilyn Manson, could we?

Dr. Drew: There are a lot of theories. One is that it's contagious, as though it's a thought that can be implanted by messages on a CD. More likely, it's basically that people have been raised in crappy families. That's one of the fundamental reasons. And the amount of substance abuse among teens: abuse plus substances equals suicide.

A lot of it has to do with the normal difficulties of the adolescent transition; it's such a part of it. The hormones surging through your body make you depressed. The whole interpersonal experience of being a teenager is depressing. Detaching from your parents, conflicts with your parents. You're just predisposed.

Q: What group is most at risk?

Dr. Drew: Adolescent homosexual males.

Q: And beyond that?

Dr. Drew: Adolescent males in general. And then anyone who was abused in some fashion during childhood. Obviously, lower socioeconomic status often results in higher levels of stress and family dysfunction, which leads to depression and suicide.

Q: What are the most common reasons for teens to feel suicidal?

Dr. Drew: We get back to a lot of depression. Suicide is a symptom of serious depression. A lot of suicide is about being angry and feeling worthless.

Adam: I've got to believe a lot of kids look at the future as somewhat bleak. It's pretty hard to kill yourself when you're heading off to some Ivy League school on a baseball scholarship. Although overdemanding and intrusive parents can be abusive and annihilating.

Dr. Drew: A lot of it is also about relationships with other people. "Nobody talks to me. People make fun of me. I don't look right. I'm not worthwhile." And how do you decide if you're worthwhile? By the way other people treat you. So if Mom beat you up and Dad beat you up and you feel nobody else likes you, things start to look pretty dark.

Adam: I also think some of it is payback to Mom and Dad. You're going to pay them back for not paying attention to you—and boy, aren't you going to make them sorry?

Dr. Drew: As though you would be around to watch it happen and be gratified by it after you've killed yourself.

Adam: A little catch-22 going on there.

Q: What should you do if you see symptoms in someone close to you who's depressed and talking about suicide?

Dr. Drew: Always take it very seriously. Tell an adult. Make sure the people around them are aware of how they're feeling. If they actually have a plan for suicide, make sure the authorities are notified. If you see somebody starting to give away their things and looking like they're making a plan, well, people can be held against their will in hospitals or other facilities if they're acutely suicidal. Usually those suicidal feelings will pass.

Sometimes a person's life can be saved by medication and professional intervention.

Adam: You could say there are always going to be a certain percentage of people on this earth who don't want to be here and who will not be denied their suicide. I don't know if that is ever going to go away.

But there are also a lot of people who are on the fence, who could go either way. So it's the job of the people around them—teachers, parents, brothers, sisters, friends—to get involved to help them make the right decision.

Dr. Drew: Depression is treatable—and it usually gets better.

How to Help a Friend... *who is depressed or suicidal*

Dr. Drew: In terms of suicide, you can never assume that somebody is just trying to get attention. You must take it very, very seriously whenever you hear somebody talk about suicide. You should understand that this is taken with such seriousness in the medical profession that somebody with a suicidal plan would probably be placed in a hospital for three days against their will for observation. Depression is a potentially fatal illness; you're dealing with somebody's life here. You don't take any chances. You may be able to turn it around at a time which is absolutely critical.

Adam: When you start talking about suicide to friends, you relinquish your rights. At that point, people can and should intervene.

Dr. Drew: You can't make psychiatric assessments of your friends—but you can get that person some help. You have to approach it seriously, like you're really saving somebody's life. Our experience has been that people stay your friend if you look out for them because, when they get better, they appreciate it.

Adam: Even when they're not in a good place, they still understand on some level what you're trying to do, that you're looking out for them.

Teen Suicide Statistics

- Suicide is the third leading cause of death among youth between the ages of 15 and 24.
- More than 13 of every 100,000 people between the ages of 15 and 24 committed suicide in 1990.
- Approximately 5,000 teens commit suicide every year.
- White male suicides rose 50 percent between 1970 and 1978.
- White female suicides increased 12 percent between 1970 and 1978.
- The suicide rate for young blacks is also increasing.
- Cluster suicides (one suicide triggers several others) have increased within a group, such as a school or community.

(*Source: Office of Prevention, Texas Youth Commission*)

22

And in Conclusion . . .

Q: What's the toughest part of going through the teen and young-adult years?

Dr. Drew: It's leaving behind the unresolved traumas of childhood. There will never again be any opportunity to relive those experiences. They're now purely memories that the individual, no longer a child, has to resolve, at the same time that he's assimilating an adult value system. And dealing with adult biology. It's extremely painful and difficult.

Adam: I think it's uncertainty in the face of not having a well-formed identity. That's the scariest thing in the world.

It's not knowing what you're going to do for a living, if you're going to be able to afford anything, if you're going to be successful in business or relationships. And you don't have a strong base to fall back on.

You don't have much confidence. You know there's a big challenge ahead of you but you don't know if you're up to it year after year after year. At best, it's really distracting.

That's where I was at. I never knew what the hell I was going to do from one day to the next. And I never felt like I had a strong enough foundation to come off of. Most people don't have that strong family support network. People feel like they're on their own by the time they're fifteen or sixteen years old.

Dr. Drew: It's very painful. It's the point at which you have to give up all the fantasies you had during childhood, the time when your perceptions about your parents change. And you're trying to find ways to satisfy those unmet emotional needs, using your peers.

Q: How did you get through it when you were that age? How did you survive?

Adam: Fortified wine. And Nickelodeon.

Dr. Drew: At this stage in your life, other people are critical. The healthier, more intimate, and more genuine your relationships with other people, the likelier you are to maneuver through. If, God willing, your family is available, that's where you'll find meaning. If you know how to choose good friends—and most people that age don't, unfortunately—there, too, can be a source of real quality.

People don't develop emotionally without connections to other people. To the extent you're able to make connections, that gives you the capacity to move through these transitions in a fuller way.

Adam: I think you have to approach it like someone in AA: You take it one day at a time. You try to keep progressing. Don't look for the big score. Don't sit around and wait for something to happen. Be active.

Don't give yourself unrealistic goals. Just improve a little bit each day. Learn a little more about yourself; get a little more involved in what you're doing. If you're in a relationship or you're an employee, try to be a little better each day.

Time passes quickly. Before you know it, you've done a lot of work.

Q: How long did it take you to learn that?

Adam: I came up with the strategy when I was nineteen or twenty. It didn't really pay any serious dividends for a good five years—and it didn't pay any tangible monetary dividends for about ten years.

Dr. Drew: I would say take responsibility for yourself. The only thing you can change is yourself. So take responsibility for everything that happens to you. Don't blame the world or the gods or your friends, because you can't change them. If you keep blaming externals, you can never change the internals, which is ultimately the growth you need to get through this.

I remember at one point in my life feeling like there was a brick wall in front of me that went up as high as I could see. I couldn't even see the top of it. But I thought, *I have to put one peg in and then another and just start climbing this wall. I don't know how long it will take, but I'll get there if I just do it one day at a time.* And that's how I got through medical school.

Adam: The point is that you don't want to do that—and let a year go by and you're still standing there, looking up at the wall. At the end of that year, you should be at least part of the way up. It's about making progress a little bit at a time—because, over time, it adds up to something significant.

Help Lines

If you're in trouble, here are phone numbers where you can get counseling and help:

Youth Crisis Hotline	800-448-4663
Runaway Hotline	800-231-6946
Planned Parenthood	800-230-7526
Child Help USA	800-422-4453
AIDS Hotline	800-342-2437
Al-Anon for Family Members	800-356-9996 (M–F, 9 A.M.–4:30 P.M. Eastern)
Alcohol and Drug Helpline	800-821-4357
RAINN (Rape, Abuse and Incest National Network)	800-656-4673
Family Planning	800-942-1054